A Prosody Handbook

A Prosody Handbook

Karl Shapiro
The University of Nebraska

Robert Beum
The Creighton University

Harper & Row, Publishers
New York, Evanston, and London

Library of Congress Catalog Card Number: 64-24535

Poetry Acknowledgments

Several of the poems in this book are protected by copyright, and permission to reprint them or to excerpt from them has been generously granted.

The five poems by Robert Bridges are reprinted from *The Poetical Works of Robert Bridges*, The Clarendon Press, Oxford.

The poem "Still Life" by Elizabeth Daryush is reprinted from *Selected Poems of Elizabeth Daryush*, selected with a foreword by Yvor Winters, by permission of the publisher, Alan Swallow. Copyright 1948 by Elizabeth Daryush.

The poems "With Pipe and Flute," "Too Hard It Is To Sing" and "Ballad of Imitation" by Austin Dobson are taken from *The Complete Poetical Works of Austin Dobson*. Copyright 1923 by the Oxford University Press. Reprinted by permission of the Oxford University Press.

The excerpts from T. S. Eliot's poems, "Ash Wednesday" and "Gerontion" from *Collected Poems 1909–1962*, are reprinted by permission of the author and of the publisher, Harcourt, Brace & World, Inc.

The poem "Seguidilla" by Richard Wirtz Emerson is reprinted from *The Greengrocer's Son* by Richard Wirtz Emerson, by permission of the publisher, Alan Swallow. Copyright 1950 by Richard Wirtz Emerson.

The poem "The Bee" by John Fandel is reprinted by permission of the author.

The excerpt from Robert Frost's poem "Departmental" is from *Complete Poems of Robert Frost*. Copyright 1936 by Robert Frost. Copyright renewed 1964 by Lesley Frost Ballantine. Reprinted by permission of Holt, Rinehart and Winston, Inc.

The excerpt from Alfred Hayes' poem "The Slaughter-House" is from *New Poems 1944* edited by Oscar Williams. Copyright 1944 by Oscar Williams. Reprinted by permission of Crown Publishers, Inc.

The excerpt from Gerard Manley Hopkins' poem "At the Wedding March" is from *The Poems of Gerard Manley Hopkins* and is reprinted by permission of the Oxford University Press.

v

Contents

Foreword

From its first conception, *A Prosody Handbook* was ambitious. The authors wanted to produce a book on prosody that would be at once a practical manual for use in the classroom and of interest to the reader who is neither a teacher nor a student. Further, what was contemplated was a book that would be fairly comprehensive and as free from idiosyncrasy as possible (without reducing itself to tables and diagrams). Countless experiences in the classroom, as well as conversations with students, fellow teachers, and ordinary readers, demonstrated the need for such a book. Every prosody textbook or manual that had been written had long since gone out of print—unwept, perhaps, since even the best of them seemed only to repeat one another (and what they repeated was for the most part bald and superficial and academic without being intellectually cogent). One had the impression that a few earnest students went to them to glean what dim conceptions might be proffered, and that a few others went to them to score some points with term-dropping. The field lay open to ambition.

But of course strategy is easier than logistics. Like most subjects, prosody is an infinite one. As the planning and actual writing of the present book proceeded, nothing became more evident than that the ideal book would require teams and lifetimes; neither seemed available. Further, the very decision to produce not an encyclopedia nor a history, but an informal exposition designed for wide circulation, demanded that the book not run to great length, and consequently necessitated, at various points, the curtailment of discussion. The psychological advantage of brevity is never gained without cost; nevertheless, for the present undertaking it would seem to be a necessity. And yet despite the necessary pulling in of horns, the original aim of the book has not been greatly altered. It is intended to serve anyone who is interested in poetry or in poetic structure generally. It is not designed to serve as a textbook for doctoral seminars in prosody; nor is it a book for theorists themselves. The authors confess to a pragmatic bias. It is a book which the teacher ought to be able to assign as a supplementary text in any course which deals with poetry; and having assigned it, he ought to feel free to say nothing at all about prosody. If the book requires, at point after point, illumination by the teacher or from other material, it will have failed in part of its purpose.

A word about the plan of the book: In the first place, the treatment throughout is informal and selective. This will infuriate some readers, but rigorous schematizing would have disappointed others. The book will work best if it is read in its entirety and consecutively. The overall design is a working from the smaller elements to the larger: from syllables to feet to lines to stanzas, and from smaller stanzas to larger ones.

The Glossary should provide the reader with ready definitions (and in many cases with illustrations) of the more ubiquitous prosodic terms. Most of these terms are, of course, dealt with at greater length in the body of the text itself.

The section on classical prosody is intended as the merest introduction to the subject; this is a handbook of *English* prosody; but of course English prosody does not exist in a historical vacuum.

The Bibliography is intensely selective; every scholar, no doubt, will find some favorite work omitted. At the same time, it lists both books and articles, and is a larger listing than any which is widely available at present. Intrinsic merit has been the primary criterion; but a number of items have been included on the basis of popularity and historical significance. The Books/Articles division customary in bibliographies seems to the present authors largely pointless except in the case of a vast listing. As for categories, so many are possible that there might be nearly as many headings as entries; in any event, category listings are available already from countless sources; the chronological listing adopted here may be of some slight initial value to the reader who is interested in the development of prosodic scholarship.

The rather extensive material in the chapter titled Scansions and Comments will introduce the reader to numerous problems of scansion, and confront him with the necessity of considering a poem's prosody simultaneously with all its other elements and aspects.

No book was ever more indebted; what can be said? To poet, critic, scholar, teacher, editor, publisher; to Mr. G. Thomas Fairclough for valuable research assistance; to the readers who offered suggestions or took us to task; to our wives, who gave us ideas and encouragement, who typed and proofread—homage.

KARL SHAPIRO
ROBERT BEUM

A Note on Terms

Strophe, onomatopoeia, macron, iambic, catalectic, epodic—the Greek terminology that makes up the vocabulary of prosody is undoubtedly objectionable in many ways. Yet, despite a number of attempts to supplant it with a native idiom, it persists, and its very familiarity—a familiar strangeness—invites us to keep on using it. There is always the risk of inventing terms no clearer or more convenient or less "literary" than the Greek ones. "Duple rising rhythm" is English enough (though "duple" is suspect), but it is six syllables for three ("iambic"). And how are we to Anglicize "catalexis" or "epodic" without using very long, and probably equally awkward, phrases? Succinctness and a measure of familiarity are formidable advantages.

1
Prosody as a Study

Poetry—like prose, and like music—is an art of S O U N D S moving in T I M E.

For particular purposes, these sounds may be analyzed into various units; for example, into P H O N E S (the smallest distinguishable speech sounds) or, in English and in many other languages, into S Y L L A B L E S.

Traditionally, the metrical structure of English poetry—the outward and obvious features such as rhyme and meter and stanza form, that make it different from prose—has been analyzed in terms of syllables, and this remains the most useful way of proceeding.

In any case, we have a situation in which *sounds* are uttered and perceived *consecutively*. As written or spoken syllables move forward, they create images and ideas that we understand and respond to. Simultaneously, we respond also to the very sounds themselves and to the quality of their movement: their relative speed or slowness, and any patterns of regularity, or relative regularity, they may form. The stream of sound turns into images and thoughts and feelings; but it also registers in its own right.

I

Poetry, then, like music, is primarily a temporal art, rather than a plastic art like painting or sculpture. Sound, its movement and pattern, is at the very heart of a poem; it is part of the poet's technique, and as important in determining our imaginative and emotional responses to a poem as are the meanings of the words themselves. It might make the point to say that a poet's prosody—his control of the stream of sound—is his language within a language. Dante Gabriel Rossetti once put the idea memorably and much more strongly: "Color and meter, these are the true patents of nobility in painting and poetry, taking precedence of all intellectual claims."

A poet's intention always is to shape a prosodic form that is perfectly suited to the point he wants to make—to the particular quality of human experience he deals with—in this particular poem. Usually, he creates a form that "says" the same thing as the words themselves say: the prosody complements the poem's thought and feeling, helping to fuse all the various elements into an indivisible and compelling experience. The hardy stresses, rapid rhythms, and playful rhymes of

> Hey diddle diddle, the cat and the fiddle,
> The cow jumped over the moon;
> The little dog laughed to see such sport,
> And the dish ran away with the spoon!

are wonderfully appropriate to the madcap action, the delightful nonsense and raucous tone, of the verse; a metric very different but equally expressive would be expected in a meditative or elegiac poem.

Sometimes the wedding of sound and sense takes a rather different aspect. In order to gain an ironic or amusing effect, a poet may shape a prosodic form that qualifies—perhaps contradicts—rather than reinforces the sense. In the sonnet by Sir Philip Sidney beginning, "Loving in truth, and fain in verse my love to show," the lover complains he is at his wit's end to write a poem that will favorably impress his mistress. At last he hears what seems to be sound advice from his muse:

> Fool, said my muse to me, look in thy heart and write.

But the very choice of the elaborate and difficult form—a hexameter sonnet—is at odds with the muse's recommendation of an artless and reportorial approach. And so considering the poem as a prosodically shaped thing, as well as a network of ideas and attitudes, we see Sidney's ultimate message: art, besides sincerity and deep feeling, is necessary to the lover's success. To avoid misreading the poem or condemning it as a case of manner violating matter, the sense must be read carefully against the prosody. Taken together, the words and the metric coalesce into just the sort of coherent and witty poem that might win the lady.

In any case, a vital relationship exists between a poem's vision and its versification: the latter is in some way always made to work actively in the former's service.

To study prosody, then, is to study such things as tempo and sound, pause and flow, line and stanza, rhyme and rhymelessness. To understand and appreciate poetry *as an art*, it is as necessary to study these matters as it is to study metaphor, imagery, and connotation. It is true, of course, that the study of prosody is not essential to the immediate appreciation of a poem. Children love and understand the quite complex poems of childhood, and the adult reader may respond deeply to a poem by Frost or Herbert without knowing the mechanics or terminology of its metric. To study prosody is to go beyond immediate appreciation and to try to discover some of the means by which poetry produces its particular effects. Prosody is for those who wish to go behind the scenes. It leads to an *intellectual* appreciation, and is a necessary study for anyone who is to be considered "educated" in the art of poetry, whether he writes it or not. In the same way, a person is trained to "read" a musical score or even a painting (that is, to know the crafts of drawing, perspective, color, and mass), though the listener and viewer simply rely upon the total impact of the work. In recent decades, the study of poetry has focused intensively on the S E M A N T I C elements of the poem, and prosody has been somewhat neglected. Between the analyses of critics whose main interest lies in allusiveness and connotation, and of critics who are interested primarily in "myth" or in the "history of ideas," the M E D I U M of poetry—the moving sound stream, the song-stuff—has become an unfashionable subject. One would almost think that images and ideas somehow get expressed without a medium of expression. And yet, Shakespeare's verse shows a general pattern of

Ti-TUM | Ti-TUM | Ti-TUM | Ti-TUM | Ti-TUM

So long | as men | can breathe | or eyes | can see,

and the student of poetry is at last obliged to ask: What is the meaning of this ten-syllable standard? Why didn't Shakespeare use a twelve-syllable standard, like the French poets? Or why not a line whose fundamental pattern is the reverse: TUM-Ti | TUM-Ti | TUM-Ti | TUM-Ti | TUM-Ti? And what was the point of measuring the verse at all? It is here that we must turn to the prosodist. Any more than casual reading of poetry will inevitably give rise to questions that can only be answered—if they can be answered at all—by a study of the physical qualities of the medium itself.

And, once begun, how should such a study proceed? Where lies its end? How minutely and scientifically should one scrutinize those sounds and the patterns they make as they cut their way across time—how much knowledge makes one "educated"? Dogmatic opinions are readily available, but ultimately every reader must answer such questions for himself. A poem yields up its meaning, and makes that meaning an experience, in two ways: (1) through the semantic content of words as these are organized in sequences of images, ideas, and logical or conventional connections; and (2) through the "music," the purely physical qualities of the medium itself, such as sound color, pitch, stress, line length, tempo. Either study proves to be inexhaustible—the more so, since the matter and the metric are ultimately inseparable. Because the domain of prosody includes all that remains after the semantic content has as far as possible been excluded, *every* physical detail and aspect of a poem stands open to analysis. Traditionally, however, prosodists have limited their analyses usually to the more obvious and easily accessible features of the medium: the pattern of weaker and stronger stresses; the pauses (or lack of them) within lines and at the ends of lines; the rhyme words and rhyme pattern; line length; and the more obvious acoustic features such as euphony, dissonance, or onomatopoeia. These are analyzable in themselves and also in their relationships with the larger units of presentation: the sentence, the stanza, the whole poem. The degree of rigorousness of any such investigation depends of course on one's particular aim with a particular poem.

In time perhaps a new system of prosodic analysis, and a new terminology, will appear and become as viable as the old and familiar apparatus. Meanwhile, the traditional approach remains immensely useful, even for very sophisticated purposes, and has been followed throughout the present book.

2
Poetry and Verse

When poetry shows—as it need not—some sort of definite regularity in prosodic form—some pattern of lines, pitches, quantities, or stresses, for example—the result is V E R S E.

The term verse is sometimes used by critics to denote an inferior type of poetry ("mere verse"), but that definition is not to the purpose here. In the singular, "a verse," it refers to a single line of a poem; and by extension it sometimes means a stanza or a whole poem or a section of a chapter in the Bible. These meanings too will not be useful here. We take verse to mean simply *metered language:* that is, language in which some quality of the syllables, such as stress or quantity, is either strictly or at least relatively regularized. The determinate pattern is called M E T E R; the resulting kind of poetry is verse.

Much of the world's poetry is verse: the *Iliad* and the *Odyssey*, the tragedies of the Greeks and of Shakespeare, the *Divine Comedy* of Dante, the poems of Yeats and Frost. Some of its greatest poetry, however, lacks meter: the King James version of the Psalms (and, for that matter, the Psalms in the original Hebrew) and the poems of Walt Whitman, for example. All F R E E V E R S E is unmetered. Generally speaking, all poetry can be divided prosodically into two types: metered poetry (verse) and free verse. (Whether poetry is metrical or not has of course no bearing on its merit; Whitman's verse, for example, is greatly inferior to his *vers libre*.)

EXAMPLES

(i)

This is poetry, but not verse. There are many parallels, from sentence to sentence and within the sentences, in form and meaning; but there is no fixed pattern of line, sound, or stress.

The heavens declare the glory of God; and the firmament showeth his handywork.

Day unto day uttereth speech, and night unto night sheweth knowledge.

There is no speech nor language where their voice is not heard.

Their line is gone out through all the earth, and their words to the end of the world. In them hath he set a tabernacle for the sun.

Which is as a bridegroom coming out of his chamber, and rejoiceth as a strong man to run a race. . . .

—*Psalms:* 19, KJV

(ii)

This is poetry in the form of verse.

Whenas in silks my Julia goes,
Then, then, methinks, how sweetly flows
The liquefaction of her clothes.

Next, when I cast mine eyes and see
That brave vibration each way free,
O, how that glittering taketh me!

—HERRICK, "Upon Julia's Clothes"

(iii)

This is verse, but no one would call it poetry. It is prose imposed upon by arithmetic.

The meter makes the verse, but not, of course,
The poem, which demands much more than mere
Arithmetic; and this distinction's not
An unimportant one, since verse sometimes
Is thought sufficient or essential form.

—ANONYMOUS

3
Syllables: Color, Stress, Quantity, Pitch

A SYLLABLE is a unit of speech sound that may be uttered with a single impulse of the breath (by impulse is meant an expulsion of breath). It consists of one or more distinctive sounds, called PHONES, one of which has relatively great sonority (deep, resonant sound). Modern linguistic studies are inclined to regard the syllable as an elusive and otherwise inconvenient unit; more minutely measurable units of speech sound—the phone, the phoneme—are preferred. But English is a *stress* language, and stress is intimately bound up with the syllable; also, tradition and universal practice in literature still dictate the syllabic unit as the most practical one for prosodic analysis.

The word *ah* consists of a single syllable and a single distinctive sound or phone. The word *Amen* contains two syllables, the second of which, *-men*, has three distinctly different sounds: the consonant *m*, the short vowel *e* (ĕ), and the consonant *n*.

In English poetry four characteristics of the syllable are important: (1) COLOR, or phone quality—sometimes called TIMBRE;

8

(2) S T R E S S, or relative force or loudness; (3) Q U A N T I T Y, or time in utterance—sometimes called D U R A T I O N; and (4) P I T C H, the quality of sound determined by the frequency of the vocal vibration. S I L E N C E, or P A U S E—the absence or relative absence of sound between words or syllables—may be longer or shorter; it too, of course, is an important matter.

Here are two syllables that are also two words; for convenience, let us imagine them as beginning a sentence—

It sprawls . . .

The two words are quite different in sound color; in fact, they have no color at all in common. The stress is different too: *It* is weakly stressed relative to *sprawls*, which is forcefully attacked. The quantity is also different: *sprawls* takes much more time in utterance than *It*. And finally, the pitch is different: we raise the voice (increase the speed of our vocal vibration) on *sprawls*, bringing it "up" in pitch.

Let us examine these syllabic characteristics more closely to see what accounts for their verse-making and poetry-making powers.

I.   COLOR

S O U N D designates a vibrational energy that produces auditory sensation. C O L O R (or sound color) refers to the quality of sounds that is determined by the instrument—the vibrating material and its form—and by the medium through which the sound travels to reach the ear. The human vocal mechanism is one of the most intricate and flexible of sound-producing instruments; and poetry utilizes the resources of sound more subtly and more thoroughly than any other kind of discourse. In poetry, sound often boldly reinforces the meaning:

It was a lover and his lass,
    With a hey, and a ho, and a hey nonino,
That o'er the green corn-field did pass
    In the spring time, the only pretty ring time,
When birds do sing, hey ding a ding, ding;
Sweet lovers love the spring.

Hey, ho, hey nonino . . . hey ding a ding, ding have little semantic content, as words or syllables, *per se;* yet in the context of Shakespeare's lyric—simply as sounds—they are able to express a mood of joy and lightheartedness.

More frequently, a poet searches for sounds which will make his meaning vivid, and which at the same time will be words whose meanings the reader already knows:

> Forlorn! the very word is like a bell
> To toll me back from thee to my sole self!

Forlorn, toll, sole, and even *word* and *self* are each related to the sound or the meaning of *bell*—in this case a deep and mournful bell that reminds the poet of oncoming death.

The English language is very rich in possibilities of sound color. Following are some of the categories most frequently exploited by our poets.

1. *Resonance.*   In the present book we use this term stipulatively to mean prolongation and fullness of sound. The sounds *n, m, ng, z,* and *zh* (*none, maim, ring, nose, rouge*) usually produce lingering, droning, vibrant effects. The nasals (*n, m, ng*) are sometimes called H U M S.

> The moan of doves in immemorial elms,
> And murmuring of innumerable bees;
>
> ∽
>
> Sidonian virgins paid their vows and songs.

2. *Harshness.*   Includes throaty sounds, usually called V E-L A R S, made by putting the tongue back toward the soft palate: *k* and hard *g,* as in *kick* and *jug;* or hard *c,* as in *cough.* Synonyms are D I S S O N A N C E, C A C O P H O N Y.

> Blue-black, lustrous, thick like horsehairs,
> —Can't I see his dead eye glow.

3. *Plosiveness.*   Sounds articulated by a sudden release and then an interruption, of breath: *b, p, t, d, g,* and *k* are often plosive. There is usually a complete stoppage of breath before the release, as in *pop.*

When thou at the random grim forge, powerful amidst peers,
Didst fettle for the great grey drayhorse his bright and battering
   sandal!

These lines, celebrating a blacksmith's life, enact in language the
plosive and percussive sounds of the forge and the anvil; they attempt
of course only to suggest, not to reproduce, such noises.

4. *Breathiness.* There is a wide range of sounds—it includes
the groups known to linguists as ASPIRATES, SIBILANTS, and
FRICATIVES—that are especially suitable in contexts that seek to
create images of such qualities as breathlessness or hissing or whispering. The aspirate *h* perhaps should be considered separately. It
may be employed to create a suggestion of breathlessness, as in fatigue
or wonder or exaltation:

From harmony, from heav'nly harmony . . .

Voiceless DENTALS (*f*, and *th* as in *th*in) and voiceless sibilants (*s*
as in *s*ea, *sh* as in *sh*rew, and *ch* as in su*ch*) are made by the release
of breath through a narrow opening of the teeth or lips. In the following lines by Christopher Marlowe notice how the pattern of color
complements the sportive marine imagery:

Sweet singing mermaids sported with their loves
On heaps of heavy gold, and took great pleasure
To spurn in careless sort the shipwreck treasure.

At the beginning of Act V of *The Merchant of Venice* Shakespeare
loads his dialogue with such colors. The incidence of so many
breathy syllables lends the poetry a music appropriate to young
lovers speaking softly and wittily about the night and about other
such nights:

The moon shines bright In such a night as this,
When the sweet wind did gently kiss the trees
And they did make no noise, in such a night
Troilus methinks mounted the Trojan walls,
And sigh'd his soul toward the Grecian tents,
Where Cressid lay that night. . . .

> In such a night
> Stood Dido with a willow in her hand
> Upon the wild sea-banks, and waft her love
> To come again to Carthage.

5. Liquidity. This is the effect of certain nonfrictional and vowel-like consonants, chiefly *l* and *r*. *W* is another mild consonantal sound. These melodic consonants can help a poet build a resonant musical line. They are frequently conjoined with resonants:

> Or summer wading in a willowy run.

Here is an epigram by Herrick which uses such colors expressively:

> So smooth, so sweet, so silv'ry is thy voice,
> As, could they hear, the Damn'd would make no noise,
> But listen to thee, (walking in thy chamber)
> Making melodious words, to Lutes of Amber.

The voiced sounds *l*, *r*, *y*, *w*, *m*, and *n* may be grouped together and called SONORANTS.

One must also take the *vowels* into account. A great preponderance of vowels over consonants—especially of long and open vowels and long diphthongs—almost always produces a kind of softness somewhat different in quality from the softness that may be created by resonant or breathy or liquid consonants. A preponderance of long vowels and diphthongs often produces an effect of dignity or somberness or deliberateness:

> It was no dream; I lay broad waking.

Onomatopoeia

The whole subject of "expressive" sound or sound-painting or onomatopoeia is complicated, involving often misunderstanding and even controversy. Perhaps the best way to approach the matter is first of all to make a distinction between onomatopoeic, also called "echoic" or "imitative," *words* and a more general or diffuse kind of onomatopoeia.

Everyone recognizes the existence of certain words whose sound suggests their meaning or some aspect of their meaning: *pop, zing, cuckoo, swoosh. Swoosh* is closer to the sound made by a swooshing object than is, say, *ipk*. The word *sprawl* is slightly suggestive of the word's meaning: the extreme length or quantity of the syllable corresponds to the idea of extension or spreading. There is no quarrel over the presence of such acoustic suggestiveness in certain words.

But word onomatopoeia can rarely serve as more than the spice in the meat of a poem. The number of distinctly imitative words in English and in most other languages is quite limited, and so for this reason alone word onomatopoeia is a special effect, not a main-stay of the poet's art.

More significant, and more controversial, is a broader kind of onomatopoeia or sound-painting. A given poem, or any part of a poem, might aim at one or both of two effects: (1) the suggesting of *natural sounds*—the clangor of a brass band, the droning of bees or gnats, the lulling trickle of water—not by single words, but by repeating certain sounds so that they dominate the line or passage; (2) the suggesting of *physical qualities* other than sound, or physical processes, or even psychological states—spaciousness, slow or hesi-tant movement, celerity or agility, tension or anxiety, blustering or babbling—by making certain kinds of sounds prominent by repe-tition or by position.

There can be no doubt that poets aim at imitative effects, at creating a physical texture that *enacts* the meaning as well as states it. At one point in the eleventh song from *The Princess*, Tennyson wants us to feel that we are in the very presence of the uncongenial waters of barren mountains; an oppressive sensation of delay and purpose-lessness haunts the ledges with

> Their thousand wreaths of dangling water-smoke.

The very slow tempo of this line, achieved by long vowels and diph-thongs and resonant colors, is calculated to work actively on our sensibilities. Milton, in one line of *Comus*, wants precisely the opposite effect:

> Swift as the sparkle of a glancing star.

Here the collocation of short vowels, the striking alliteration, the lack of resonance and other tempo-slowing qualities produce a line that seems as swift as its image. "The sound must seem an Echo to the sense," Pope declared.

Certain critics and linguists have questioned, however, whether sound can really be expressive. John Crowe Ransom, I. A. Richards, and Seymour Chatman, for example, are inclined to believe that the suggestive powers of verbal sound are slight or nonexistent. They point out that the same or highly similar patterns of sound render different effects in different contexts, and they doubt, therefore, that particular sounds suggest particular qualities.

Yet even writers skeptical of acoustic expressiveness are willing to grant that Poe in the line,

> And the silken, sad, uncertain rustling of each purple curtain,

is trying to suggest the rustling sound of curtains moving in the breeze; but they would claim that the potency of the line—it *is* a vivid, a striking, line if a little mechanical (and partly perhaps because it *is* rather mechanical)—stems from the particularity and appropriateness of the meanings of the words, and that our claim to hear the rustling in the *ss* is only an afterthought. If the sibilance here suggests a rustling sound, then how is it that in other lines collocations of *ss* suggest (at least by afterthought) quite different natural sounds? For example, hissing, as in this line:

> The hissing of those vipers, forks that sass.

And the first of the following two lines from George Herbert's poem "The Church-floore" actually contains more sibilance than either of the lines above, yet they fail to suggest anything, and apparently are not intended to do so:

> Hither sometimes Sinne steals, and stains
> The marble's neat and curious veins.

The way out of this dilemma seems, however, to the present authors clear enough.

In the first place, certain sounds—the voiceless *s*, for example —possess a *range of potential* suggestibility, rather than a fixed or single capability. Thus, a prominence of *ss* is capable of suggesting certain classes of natural sounds (rustling, hissing, sighing, whispering) but not other classes (booming, humming, hammering, or groaning).

In the second place, this power of suggesting natural sounds or other qualities is relatively *weak*—too weak to operate unsupported by meaning—and because of its range, is only *latent*. The semantic content of words has to activate and focus this imitative potential. If the semantic element does not do this, then the collocations of sounds are in most cases merely neutral.

The texture of sound in most poetry, as in most prose, is merely appropriate. Meaning does, however, activate acoustic suggestiveness when there is a relationship capable of being exploited. A line full of *s*s that gives us an image of hissing is bound to focus its own sound pattern for us. If, on the other hand, sound patterns are not at all descriptive of their logical contents, then (assuming that the substitutions were normal forms) the line,

> The hibbing of those vipern, lorke that quann,

would be as potent as the original—but it patently is not.

A harsh, tongue-twisting sequence of sounds would hardly be appropriate in a context of pleasant images and indolent sensations. The slow tempos and the generally euphonious quality of Tennyson's "The Lotos-Eaters" are perfectly expressive of the island's drowsy atmosphere and of the languidness of Ulysses' men. Acoustic expressiveness is as much a fact as the fact of T E M P O. And it works in much the same way. We tend to read a passage—whether it be verse or prose is of no consequence—more slowly if the *sense* of the passage gives us images of languidness or lethargy, more quickly if the passage describes an exciting race or any rapid development; at the same time, the tempo of the passage is influenced by such physical qualities as syllable length, stress distribution, and ease of utterance.

In the vast majority of poems and parts of poems, no specific imitativeness, no enactment, is intended, and we perceive the sound pattern as merely pleasant or not unsuitable. In Ransom's words, the poet usually finds that his job is only to secure "the common genius of the language, and some degree of euphony, which is easily obtained, and otherwise have no great concern with phonetic projects."

But of course the exceptions are sometimes the most vital moments of English poetry.

Each of the three passages below is representational (expressive, onomatopoeic) in its sound:

(*i*)   Hear the loud alarum bells—
                              Brazen bells!
        What a tale of terror now their turbulency tells!
          In the startled ear of night
          How they scream out their affright!
            Too much horrified to speak,
            They can only shriek, shriek,
               Out of tune.

(*ii*)

        Whenas in silks my Julia goes,
        Then, then, methinks, how sweetly flows
        The liquefaction of her clothes.

(*iii*)   Once again
        Do I behold these steep and lofty cliffs,
        That on a wild secluded scene impress
        Thoughts of a more deep seclusion; and connect
        The landscape with the quiet of the sky.

    (*i*) In this passage by Poe the color is all-important: it has become the poet's chief means of suggesting bells ringing harshly, dissonantly. Poe works into his lines a great many somber *m*s and *n*s, hard *d*s and *k*s, exploding *t*s, and *f*s full of friction; while at the same time the bells themselves are continually suggested by the recurring *b*s and *l*s.

    (*ii*) We may remark in a general way the marriage of sound and sense in this stanza from Herrick's poem "Upon Julia's Clothes." Negatively speaking, there is a lack of harshness; positively, the lines are limpid. Of thirteen consonant sounds in the first line, for example, six are liquids or sibilants, and none of the other seven is a harsh sound (the *k*s in *silks* and *methinks* are softened by the following *s*s into which they glide; the *k*-sound in *liquefaction* is softened by the impressively soft *wuh*-sound following; and the *k* in *clothes* is softened by the *l*). There are five more liquids in the second line, and four in the third; in none of the lines is there a hard *d* or *g* or a spitting *t* or popping *p*. The sound, then, is quite onomatopoeic, but not in so striking a way as in the passage from Poe's "The Bells."

(*iii*) In this passage, from the opening of Wordsworth's "Tintern Abbey," there is no reason for the poet to make use of sound even as subtly as Herrick does in "Upon Julia's Clothes." Wordsworth is describing a landscape perspective, and his own sense of wonder and of wondrous memory; what he is trying to do is not much connected with color, which becomes a very subordinate matter for him. Still, what we are not likely to be aware of, he must take pains to avoid *inadvertent* effects of sound. Accidental rhyme or alliteration would tend to lead our attention away from the thoughts and images he wants to make paramount. Yet rhymes and alliteration will easily creep into one's language. Tennyson once lamented that alliteration came so spontaneously to him he was constantly forced to revise his poems to eliminate it where it added no vigor or melody but simply existed as unwanted ornament. Up to the words, "and connect," in the Wordsworth passage, sound color is pretty much balanced or evenly distributed. Although from "and connect" to the end of the passage we do find a recurring *k* (there are five *k*-sounds in all), they are far apart, and the image and idea being presented form such a dominant impression that we scarcely notice them as color. If we notice them at all, it is only because the slight connection in sound, or alliteration, seems in a very unobtrusive way to emphasize the connection between landscape and quiet day. We are not so likely to notice color in those lines of poetry in which it is not being used deliberately and actively. When an idea or visual image comes to be the center of attention, our sensitivity to sound seems to lessen a bit. And since poetry frequently deals in images and ideas that have no direct connection with sound, sound often becomes a relatively subordinate element.

II.   STRESS

Ours is an ACCENTUAL or STRESS language. When we utter a word of more than one syllable, we give one of the syllables more force or loudness than the others:

rep-u-ta-tion.

We say that *-ta-* is the stressed or accented syllable. It may be further distinguished as the P R I M A R Y S T R E S S. Among the three remaining syllables of this word, we still note a difference in *degree* of accent: *rep-* receives more vocal emphasis than *-u-* or *-tion*, and so we call it a S E C O N D A R Y S T R E S S.

Similarly, when we articulate a group of words, certain of them are made more prominent by vocal force:

(*i*)   Ours was the marsh country, down by the river, within, as the river wound, twenty miles of the sea.

(*ii*)   Beside a pumice isle in Baiae's bay.

Stress is the most prominent and most significant acoustic element in our language. In other languages—French, for example—stress is not significant; and some languages, such as classical Greek and Chinese, accomplish by P I T C H what English does by stress.

Determining which syllables in a line of verse receive the primary stresses is the first step toward S C A N N I N G the line; that is, toward discovering its metrical pattern. This initial step often gives one a great deal of trouble. In scansion there is no substitute for experience and an open mind. The student's traditional fear and trembling derive mostly from inexperience, often from the supposition that poetry is such an arcane use of language that no experience of ordinary speech or of prose can be of any assistance.

In this book, we shall mark a full or primary stress with ′, a secondary stress with ″, and a weak stress (often called a nonstress) with a dot above the syllable: ·. We do not find it useful to distinguish, in scansion, lower levels of stress. The stress marks are traditionally placed above the vowel or diphthong of the syllable; for purposes of neatness they are sometimes placed in the middle of a word or syllable:

The hoárse, róugh vérse;

The hoárse, róugh vérse.

Notice that in line (i) above, a sentence from the opening chapter of Dickens' novel *Great Expectations*, words of only one syllable are made prominent by their contexts: they are stressed because they have the more important meanings. As for words of more than one syllable, the stress falls on the same syllable on which it would fall if the word were isolated, as in a dictionary. The same principles apply to verse. The best way to begin scanning is to go through the lines and mark stresses simply as they are dictated by sense and, in the case of words of more than one syllable, by the customary or L E X I C A L stress. Many words—especially nouns and verbs—that designate concrete and humanly most significant things, qualities, or actions almost always receive a stress: *man, girl, heart, child, love, day, night, earth, star, sing, drive, beat, move, go, find,* etc.

Metrical position may cause a word to receive greater or lesser stress than it would normally obtain:

Sylvia the fair, in the bloom of fifteen,

Felt an in|nocent warmth | as she lay | on the green;
She had heard of a pleasure, and something she guessed
By the towzing, and tumbling, and touching her breast.

She saw | the men eag|er, but was | at a loss,

What they meant | by their sighing, and kissing so close.

In these lines, metrical position causes the normally stressed *Felt* and *What* to be weak; and *was* in the fifth line receives a stress it would not ordinarily obtain. Here is another example:

"I am of Ireland
And the Holy Land of Ireland,

And time | runs on," | cried she.

Because of its position in the line, *she* receives a stress. In the normal word order ("And time runs on," she cried) there would be a stress on *cried* rather than on the pronoun.

Articles, prepositions, and conjunctions are usually unstressed, but there are exceptions. The metrical pattern of the following line, for example, is very common:

$$\text{i sáw | him háp|py ín | the wóod.}$$

The stress on *in* is not nearly as forceful as the other three stresses; yet in relationship to -*py* and *the*, the preceding and following syllables, it does achieve prominence. It gets this accentual prominence perhaps as much from custom as from metrical position; in such a construction, whether it occur in verse or in prose, we stress the preposition. The same is true of the example from "I Am of Ireland";

even in prose, custom or convention would demand *cried she*, rather than *cried she*.

The existence of degrees of stress has important ramifications: since the degree varies from point to point, even a sequence of lines that are metrically very regular will often avoid monotony. English poetry is rhythmically richer, thanks to the nonuniformity of stress.

Achieving a memorable rhythm—in poetry as in prose—is an art that requires both patience and gifts. But there is nothing mysterious about the process of making meter. To meter language is nothing more than to take a group of words and put them together in such a way that a distinct sequence of relatively stressed and relatively unstressed syllables results:

(*i*)

whiskey
ice
amber
glass
the
the
and
fill

(*ii*)

$$\text{Whiskey and the ice fill the amber glass.}$$

(iii)

The íce and whískey fíll the ámber gláss.

In lines of poetry perhaps the most important uses of stress are these: (1) to create meter and/or rhythm; (2) to avoid monotony; (3) to change tempo; (4) to intensify meaning at a particular point. Saving for a later chapter the complex question of meter and rhythm, let us look briefly at each of the other three functions.

Here are some lines from Wordsworth:

> To look on nature, not as in the hour
> Of thoughtless youth; but hearing oftentimes
> The still, sad music of humanity,
> Nor harsh nor grating, though of ample power
> To chasten and subdue.

Simple mechanical manipulations will reveal what a vital part the stress pattern plays:

> To look on nature, not as in the hour
> Of thoughtless youth; but oftentimes hearing
> The music of humanity: sad, still,
> Nor grating nor harsh, though of ample power
> To subdue and chasten.

Without changing the line pattern and without altering the passage's basic meaning, changing a few sequences of words has destroyed the meter—the relatively regular sequence of weaker and stronger stresses—and created uninteresting rhythms. What meter is left is too feeble to make itself felt. If we meant by these changes to introduce variety into the passage, we have introduced far too much of it. The original passage itself contains several variations that allow it to avoid the stiffness and monotony that would result from perfect regularity. For example, in the third line there are three successive beats *(still, sad mus-)*; and in the fifth line, the fourth syllable, *and*, is a nonstress although it falls theoretically in a stress position (at best it receives a secondary stress). These are only two instances of a number of variations Wordsworth plays on the hypothetical pattern of ·/·/·/·/·/.

Notice too that the three consecutive stresses of the third line create a certain *emphasis*. They help direct our attention to the idea of the continuing history of human sorrow, which is the key idea of the whole passage.

At the same time, these three beats coming together slow down the *tempo* of the line; and, of course, that slowing is effective and appropriate to the sense, which is dignified and poignant.

There are other important points about stress:

1. A line containing several strong beats will ordinarily seem more vigorous, more packed with energy and meaning, than a line equally long but short on well-stressed syllables. Compare the impressive

> Bare ruin'd choirs, where late the sweet birds sang

with

> The melancholy slackening that ensued.

2. So prevalent is stress in English, that in any meaningful sequence of words we rarely find more than two, and almost never more than three, successive nonstresses. And the rhythm of a sequence of words in which primary stresses are separated by intervals of three or four nonstresses is usually flat or limp, casual and uninteresting. We are habituated to stress; we depend on it, and are disappointed almost viscerally when it is sparse. None of this would hold true, however, for a language in which stress is weaker than in English (for example, as we have noted before, modern French and classical Greek).

3. As we read a line of verse, we are unconsciously so eager, as it were, to get to a primary stress, that we tend to race past the weaker syllables. Such a stress sequence as the following, then, is not likely to be suitable for expressing patient endurance, suffering, or serious protest; or for any grave, dignified, or poignant feeling:

../../../../.

The rhythm is likely to speed or lilt, to sway or trip along.

4. A number of strong stresses coming in succession will usually slow the tempo of a line. We have already noticed such a slowing in Wordsworth's "still, sad music." Here is another example:

As a dare-gale skylark scanted in a dull cage

Man's mounting spirit in his bone-house, mean house, dwells—

The laborious effect in these lines from Gerard Manley Hopkins' sonnet "The Caged Skylark" suggests physically the idea of man's confined and hampered—"caged"—spirit.

5. When the pattern of stresses and nonstresses is almost perfectly regular but achieves beauty rather than monotony, it tends to establish a tone that is dignified, exalted, or otherwise very emphatic. In Act V of Shakespeare's play *Antony and Cleopatra*, Cleopatra resolves:

Give me my robe, put on my crown. I have

Immortal longings in me. Now no more

The juice of Egypt's grape shall moist this lip.

The stress pattern is almost perfectly regular: $\cdot\prime$ or $\prime\prime\prime$.

III.   QUANTITY

Syllables are relatively LONG or SHORT, according to the time it takes to utter them. It takes less time to say *it* than to say *sprawls*.

Syllable QUANTITY or DURATION is relative: *him* is short compared with *thing*, but long if compared with the snappier *it*; and *thing* is probably not as long as *sprawls*.

Quantity is much more difficult to determine than stress, and the presence of powerful stress in English tends to obscure it. It is nonetheless important, because it influences *tempo* and consequently influences rhythm.

In English we have no exactly defined principle we can apply to determine whether a syllable is long or short. *Sprawls* is no doubt one of the longest syllables in our language, and *it* one of the shortest; but, as we have already noted, the whole matter is quite relative. In practice, however, we are sensitive to tempo; there is no gain-saying the fact that certain lines of verse, or parts of lines, move much more slowly than others; and by physical law, long syllables tend to slow the tempo.

What combinations of sounds tend to make a syllable *long?* At least three: (1) the presence of a resonant or of a sibilant color (*sing*, *stash*, *rungs*, *hiss*); (2) the presence of a long vowel or of a long diphthong (h*o*pe, sc*e*ne, v*oi*d, h*ou*se); (3) the presence of clusters of sounded consonants (*script*, *crunched*). Other things being equal, short syllables speed up the tempo of a line, and long ones slow it down.

Note in the following examples how much more quickly Shakespeare's line (*i*) goes by than Milton's (*ii*), although each one contains a pause and is built on the same stress pattern:

(*i*)　　Tell me, where is fancy bred?

(*ii*)　　Nymphs˝and shepherds, dance no more.

Sibilant colors and resonant *m*s and *n*s draw the second line out. The tempo matches the sense in each case: Shakespeare's tone is light and playful, Milton's more sober and deliberate.

We noticed this line of Sir Thomas Wyatt's earlier:

It was no dream, I lay broad waking.

A strong pause, of course, helps to slow the line, but its adagio tempo is due even more to the long vowels and to resonance. The slow, dignified movement is wonderfully expressive of the speaker's mood: here is a lover, now out of favor, experiencing all the poignancy of turning about clearly and deliberately in his memory the romantic details of a tryst.

Quantity becomes onomatopoeic in a similar way in the opening line of Henry Vaughan's poem "The Waterfall":

With what deep murmurs through time's silent stealth.

Here again the numerous long syllables (marked with MACRONS) slow the line and suggest the eddy and backwater of the river as it approaches the falls.

Like stress and color, then, quantity can become an echo to the sense. Of English poets, perhaps Milton, Tennyson, Swinburne, and Bridges were the most conscious of quantity and the most successful in putting it to various effective uses.

In English more frequently than not a stressed syllable will at the same time be a long syllable. Notice how length and stress coincide in Pope's line:

The glance by day, the whisper in the dark.

But not infrequently the opposite situation prevails. In the line below, from a song in John Fletcher's play *Valentinian*, notice that in at least two instances stress and length do not coincide (the second syllables of *hollow* and *silver* are surely at least as long as the first—and probably longer):

Like hollow murmuring wind or silver rain.

The rhythm of a line of poetry—that is, the total, unique quality of its movement—will obviously be influenced not only by quantity alone, but also by the relationship between quantity and stress. Once again, it is interesting to note that the possible wide variations in syllable length and in degree of stress *as the two conjoin* make for variety and subtlety in English rhythm.

IV.   PITCH

The PITCH of a syllable, like that of a musical tone, means the relative highness or lowness of its sound; or, technically, the frequency of the vocal vibration.

In certain Oriental verse, the metrical pattern is in part the pattern of varying pitches. Although not such a structural element in English verse, pitch is a prominent quality of any English utterance, and so necessarily influences our response to any kind of discourse.

Stress and a rise in pitch, like stress and lengthened quantity, tend to coincide. The primary stresses in a line of English verse are also usually points of ascending pitch. This rise is merely a normal characteristic of our language: it does not signal changes in meaning. The main use of pitch in English is, of course, to convey by contrasts our attitudes.

The coinciding of stress and raised pitch, of weak stress and lowered pitch, becomes particularly important at the end of a verse line, which is rhetorically a point of considerable prominence. (Other things being equal, words placed at the beginning or at the end of a unit of discourse—be it phrase, clause, sentence, line—are likely to draw greater attention than words placed in between.) A line that terminates on an unstressed syllable normally drops in pitch; there is thus quite a falling off of energy. Lines so terminating are called F E M I N I N E and may be rhymed or unrhymed. Lines that end on a stressed syllable are called M A S C U L I N E. Unless we are insensitive to the qualities of sound, we register a distinctly different impression in each case. This is all the more true because tradition has taught us to *expect* the masculine rather than the feminine ending. (In Italian our expectation would be the other way around.) In any event, the quietness of a feminine ending lends itself to a certain expressiveness: a poet may use it to help convey softness of feeling, hesitancy, a lingering of thought, or similar qualities. Notice, for example, the appropriateness of the feminine terminations in Hamlet's most famous soliloquy:

> To be or not to be, that is the question
> Whether 'tis nobler in the mind to suffer
> The slings and arrows of outrageous fortune . . .

The extra unstressed syllable at the end of each line allows the prince to drop his voice—as he well might in his melancholy and reflectiveness. The following passage also makes use of the feminine line's expressive ending:

> For her discourse, it is so full of rapture,
> You only will begin then to be sorry
> When she doth end her speech, and wish, in wonder . . .

In a prosody in which feminine endings are the rule—as they are in Italian—the ear is so accustomed to the "drop" that there is no tendency to associate it with "weak" actions or qualities.

4
The Foot

(i)   That time of year thou may'st in me behold
        When yellow leaves, or none, or few, do hang
        Upon those boughs which shake against the cold.

(ii)   The Assyrian came down like the wolf on the fold,
        And his cohorts were gleaming in purple and gold;
        And the sheen of their spears was like stars on the sea.

(iii)   Straight mine eye hath caught new pleasures
        Whilst the landscape round it measures:
        Russet lawns and fallows gray,
        Where the nibbling flocks do stray.

(iv)   Down in the valleys the shadows are thickening;
        Stars coming on and the lights of the houses . . .

What makes all of these passages verse is the unmistakable regularity they show in the distribution of stressed and unstressed— or, more strictly speaking, strongly and less strongly stressed— syllables.

In (*i*), the even-numbered syllables receive a stronger beat than the odd-numbered ones:

That time of year thou may'st in me behold.

In the lines of (*iii*), the pattern is reversed:

Straight mine eye hath caught new pleasures.

In the lines of (*ii*), every stressed syllable is preceded by two unstressed ones:

And the sheen of their spears was like stars on the sea.

This pattern is exactly reversed in (*iv*):

Down in the valleys the shadows are thickening.

In each case, the words have been so ordered as to make *sense;* they have also been arranged so that their accents make a definite *pattern.* To repeat a point we made earlier: words in verse usually retain the same accents they have in prose, in conversation, or in the dictionary. If a line of verse happens to contain monosyllables or to be composed of a succession of monosyllables ("And the sheen of their spears was like stars on the sea"), then the stresses fall both upon the words that are conventionally given vocal force and upon those that are made prominent by their contexts (these are likely to coincide).

Then, using vertical bars, we can isolate the units that make up the pattern:

That time | of year | thou may'st | in me | behold;

And the sheen | of their spears | was like stars | on the sea.

We call these units FEET. To SCAN or make a SCANSION simply means in lines of verse to determine and mark the stresses and non-stresses, and then to mark off the feet.

A perfect, or even highly regular, metrical pattern is exceptional rather than typical in English poetry. Most lines show some irregularity, and often the variance from the theoretical pattern is

very great, as in the following three lines, whose meter supposedly
in each case is, · / · / · / · / · / :

Of man's first disobedience, and the fruit;

As a dare-gale skylark scanted in a dull cage;

When to the sessions of sweet silent thought.

As the pattern becomes less regular, we have more difficulty determining just which syllables belong in which feet. For example, how
should the third line above be construed?

When to | the ses|sions of | sweet si|lent thought;

When to the | sessions of | sweet si|lent thought;

When | to the ses|sions of sweet | silent | thought.

Or does it make a great deal of difference whether we can agree on
the best scansion? Over the "correct" scansion of individual lines
and poems, critics and scholars have sometimes waged great wars in
and out of print. Unfortunately, not many of these battles have been
decisive! What about the poets themselves? Do they, in the act of
composition—which includes, of course, the act of revision—consciously or unconsciously apportion their lines in terms of feet?

Let us take the last question first. The answer to it, we feel,
is much more often a yes than a no. Once a poet decides to write in
a meter, he obliges himself to stay within it, allowing of course for
wide variations at particular points—a traditional liberty of English
verse. The poet is more or less bound to stay within a pattern once
he adopts it, for a quite simple reason: he has established a pattern,
and this means among other things that he has established an expectation in the reader or listener. The reader is induced to look for and
is thus far satisfied with continually finding a certain order. Marked
changes in that pattern establish a sense of contrast; the reader is put
on his guard. Variation beyond that which is needed for securing
rhythmic variety and now and then for a sudden emphasis brought

about by metrical surprise, makes the reader wonder why the pattern has changed; and if nothing in the sense of the verse seems to warrant it, the variance is likely to be perceived as mere irrationality or inconsistency. The poet himself, in the midst of composition, is certain to feel obliged to conform more or less continually to his adopted pattern: radical and repeated departures from the scheme are almost inevitably bound up with *changes of tone*, and the careful preservation and modulation of tone is the very essence of all successful imaginative discourse. Poems that begin as ballads keep on being ballads to the end, and iambic sonnets do not suddenly metamorphose into trochaic couplets. And so, this much at least may be said: the poet tends to adhere to his adopted pattern of stresses and nonstresses; and that pattern is susceptible to being analyzed into units or "feet," or it would not *be* a pattern.

A further point in defense of the "foot approach" begs admittance. Until quite recent times, English poets were, almost to a man, heirs of classical culture, which included classical verse and classical prosodic concepts and terminology; and their poetry invariably was born and bred on the foot. It would be foolish, then, to disregard in a modernist or intuitionist frenzy the whole business of the foot and its attendant implications. If any point in prosodic matters does *not* require debate, it is that English poets were early made and long kept acutely conscious of the classical tradition.

In answer to the other question, it must be said that it *is* important to discover the metrical pattern of verse. And, once again, for a very simple reason. The right way to read English verse is a compromise between a "natural" reading in which one delivers the verse as if it were prose or ordinary speech, simply observing conventional phrasing and logical emphases; and a metrical reading. One should neither read "sing-song," nor fail to create the sense of pattern. Verse is not prose and not extemporaneous speech; it ought to make both its love of order and its use of order felt—yet without seeming strained or mechanical. This art of compromise is a delicate one, and of course every poem poses its own problems; thus it is that few people manage to deliver verse with maximum effectiveness.

In scanning, one should look for the general metrical pattern of the whole poem or stanza, and then interpret the meter of troublesome lines in terms of that pattern. Thus, if a poem is found to be iambic, an effort should be made to give any vexing line within it an iambic interpretation. Furthermore, such a line should be analyzed in terms of that poet's habitual variations or licenses, for one poet allows an extra syllable here, but not there; elides under certain conditions only, etc. Knowing, for example, that the line,

> Ruining along the illimitable inane,

is from a poem whose meter is a pattern of ten syllables to the line, with stresses on the even-numbered syllables, we ought to hesitate before we scan it, say,

> Ruining | along | the illim|itable | inane.

The poet himself undoubtedly conceived the pattern to be

> Ruining | along | the illim|itab|le inane,

fusing by *elision* the first two syllables of *Ruining*, and fusing *the* with *il-*, and *-le* with *in-*. The poet regularly makes such fusions elsewhere.

Occasionally, a poet will change meters absolutely. Thus, the very first line of Chaucer's *Canterbury Tales* shows not the expected alternating pattern of unstressed and then stressed syllables, but the reverse of that scheme (i.e., trochaic rather than iambic):

> Whan that | Aprill | with his | shoures | sote.

In the case of lines or of whole poems so irregular as to offer a variety of defensible scansions, it is often possible to accomplish a great deal, even putting entirely aside the question of breakdown by feet. Thus, it remains important to look over the verse to see just where the beats and nonbeats fall, and then to see how these crests and troughs are related to meaning and effect. We can usually see what effects are rendered by the points of greater and lesser stress without having to analyze the line into units of feet.

For instance, it is greatly to the point to see that (1) the stresses in the Shakespeare line quoted earlier (see page 29) coincide with the words most important in meaning and feeling, (2) these stresses lend emphasis to the words, and (3) the stresses make the sibilant alliteration of *sessions*, *sweet*, and *silent* more vigorous, so that the alliteration itself becomes more emphatic.

The four verse passages that open this chapter are examples of IAMBIC, ANAPESTIC, TROCHAIC, and DACTYLIC feet respectively:

iamb (us)	the cóld
anapest	on the séa
trochee	Whére the
dactyl	thíckening

These four are the only feet used as the norm in English verse, and of these four, iambic meter is by far the most common, dactylic the rarest. Even the anapest is seldom employed without a very considerable iambic alloy, as in

The séa | is at ébb, | and the sóund | of her út|mòst wórd,

Is sóft | as the léast | wàve's lápse | in a stíll | smàll réach.

The very nature of our language, and not simply the caprice of poets, has given these four feet their dominance, and given the iambic foot dominance among them. It is in fact, as we shall see shortly, all but impossible to use any other combinations of stress and nonstress, except as variations.

Two other feet are fairly common as occasional substitutes for one of the basic four—the SPONDEE and the PYRRHIC:

spondee:

Hárd, róugh;

pyrrhic:

Of the.

But constructions such as

/ / | / / | / / | / /

or

· · | · · | · · | · ·

are barely possible in English, even theoretically. The spondaic line would have to consist almost entirely of monosyllables; we have few or no truly spondaic words in English, and any word of three or more syllables would necessarily introduce a nonstress into the line. And the theoretical pyrrhic meter would necessarily consist of a series of articles, prepositions, conjunctions, etc.; yet constructions so lacking in verbs and nouns—which would necessarily draw stresses—are inconceivable. Furthermore, in English stress is so emphatic—crests of thought and feeling tend to coincide with points of stress—that a succession of even three or four stresses is enormously impressive and may be employed only when special effects are desired. Paucity of stress, on the other hand, is so difficult for our stress-loving English voices to manage, and is to us so weak aesthetically, that we do find successions of three, four, and more stresses more frequently than we find three or four consecutive nonstresses, and of course syntax is constantly demanding the introduction of some word that is bound to draw a stress.

Even the anapest and the dactyl are difficult to manage in serious English verse, especially in verse of a meditative or philosophic cast; there is no better proof of this than the fact that, after centuries of experimentation, the good serious poems in these meters are so few. In these trisyllabic meters, the proportion of nonstresses to stresses (2 : 1) is rather unnatural—in the sense of strain. Further, the voice, eager to reach a stress, tends to race over the nonstresses; and the resulting speed, in turn, tends to lighten the tone. Consequently, these meters seem to be unsuited for the expression of qualities of feeling such as anxiety, suffering, resolve, and serenity.

Probably nine-tenths of Modern English verse—that written since, say, 1500—is iambic. Why this iambic dominance should prevail is not to be answered overhastily, especially since the iambic, or some analogue of it, is a much-favored meter by other ancient and modern languages. Various explanations have been proposed from

time to time, but the complexity of facts and possibilities has a way
of overwhelming the simplicity of theories. A very modest con-
jecture will have to suffice for the present book.

One of the distinguishing attributes of poetry is *intensity*.
Really excellent poetry either says a very great deal in a very few
words, or like much Old Testament poetry consistently reaches a
very high tone or very deep feeling, with or without actual verbal
economy. In English, as we have already pointed out, intensity of
expression is nearly always accompanied by an *abundance of stresses*.
Now, in English prose the ratio of nonstresses to stresses ranges
from about 2:1 to 3:1. This means that in the more intense language
of poetry, one should expect the ratio to be closer to 1:1, and we
find that in fact 9:7 is a common figure. Clearly, then, a balance or
near balance between troughs and crests is called for.

But of course a trochee gives us this balance as well as an
iamb. It may be that the vocabulary and syntax of modern English
run counter to trochaic meter. It is certainly true that our most
ubiquitous nouns are words of one or two syllables (in the latter the
stress usually falls on the first syllable), and that these are ordinarily
preceded by unstressed articles, prepositions, or conjunctions:

. . . a són . . . the fáther thínks

. . . in dánger, hé . . . and sóns.

There is another possible strike against the trochee. Eager as we are
in reading a line of verse to get to a stress, we may not be so eager
as to delight very often in *starting* the line with a stress. To begin lines
with stresses is perhaps too emphatic for ordinary purposes; the
physical effort required to raise pitch and force possibly ignores a
desire to anticipate the vocal intensity—to be led up to it by first
entering upon a lower level. In a long poem, trochaic verse tends to
make the first word of the line overly emphatic.

Another point is that much poetry, lyric as well as dramatic,
is intended to suggest the relatively relaxed and artless qualities of
ordinary speech, whether dialogue, as in the verse play and the
dramatic poem, or the poet's own voice. If it does strive for lin-

guistic and physiological naturalness, then iambic is ordinarily the meter best suited to its purpose: it best suggests the structures of informal speech. Greek and Roman poets explicitly recognized this suitability, and used quantitative iambic meter extensively for subjects of less than exalted character: for homely verse, for the lampoon, and for more intellectual satire. The Latin *iambus* derives from a Greek word meaning "a cripple." The short syllable represents the lame foot, the long one the foot descending with normal strength, perhaps with the added strength of the cane.

EXAMPLES

IAMBIC

(*i*)   The trampling steed, with gold and purple decked,
        Chawing the foamy bit, there fiercely stood.

(*ii*)   Wherein Leander on her quivering breast,
        Breathless spoke something, and sighed out the rest.

The first passage is from the Earl of Surrey's translation of the *Aeneid*, Book IV, and is in unrhymed iambic pentameter (five iambic feet to a line) or BLANK VERSE. The second passage is from Christopher Marlowe's exuberant amatory narrative *Hero and Leander*. Its lines add rhyme to the iambic pentameter, forming a HEROIC COUPLET.

Surrey's meter is highly regular. The only noniambic feet are *Chawing* (a trochee) and *there fierce-*, a spondee or an iamb in which the first syllable is a secondary stress.

The couplet shows considerably more variation: *on* is in a stress position but is only very lightly stressed in performance; *quivering* introduces an extra syllable into the line; the first foot of the second line is a trochee, the second a spondee; *and*, although in a stress position, is very weakly stressed, while *sighed*, in a nonstress position, receives good force. This variableness of rhythm matches the sense: the increasingly disordered meter helps vivify the lovers' loss of control in general, and their somewhat uncoordinated physical movements in particular.

(*iii*)   Since there's no help, come let us kiss and part,
      Nay, I have done; you get no more of me,
And I am glad, yea, glad with all my heart.

(*iv*)   Look homeward, Angel, now, and melt with ruth;
      And, O ye dolphins, waft the hapless youth.

These two passages illustrate the adaptability of iambic meter. In (*iii*), we have the first three lines of a sonnet by Michael Drayton. They are distinctly colloquial; we seem almost to be overhearing the speaker. But the effect, while colloquial, is not lax or pedestrian. The couplet in (*iv*) is from Milton's pastoral elegy "Lycidas." Its rhythm seems formal and lofty, as befits the subject. Notice that both passages are quite regular metrically, the Milton couplet almost perfectly so. *Highly regular meter tends to establish a formal tone.* Even Drayton's lines, though in diction they seem almost like direct speech, have, and are intended to have, a certain formal character.

(*v*)   and if one wheel had rest
    It was because the other was at work.
    The Pair had but one inmate in the house.

(*vi*)   Batter my heart, three person'd God; for, you
    As yet but knocke, breathe, shine, and seeke to mend;
    That I may rise, and stand, o'erthrow mee, and bend
    Your force, to breake, blowe, burn and make me new.

When poets wish to use iambic meter to suggest the low intensities, the homely or pedestrian qualities, of much spoken language, they are likely to violate the normal iambic pattern by distributing stresses and nonstresses irregularly, by adding extra syllables to the line, and especially *by reducing the number and strength of stresses.* Note the scarcity of strong stresses in the two full lines of (*v*), from Wordsworth's "Michael".

On the other hand, when the poet wants to suggest the vigor, the dynamic qualities, of speech, and when his attitude is not at all formal, he is likely to alter the pattern in a very different way, and his verse to show *strong and abundant stresses.* The quatrain (*vi*),

from one of Donne's Holy Sonnets, shows beside an irregular distribution of stresses, distinctly heavy ones; and all lines but the
third contain six stresses instead of the expected five.

(vii)   . . . for now a sea
           Upsurging, poured tremendous o'er the lee,
           And filled the hold; while pressed by wave and wind,
           To right and left, by turns, the ship inclined.
                                          —JUVENAL, *Satire XII*
                                          trans. William Gifford

This, we think, is a failure. All seventeen feet are perfect
iambs. Such regularity is in itself rhythmically uninteresting and
monotonous. And to make matters worse, this absolutely formal
rhythm is in direct conflict with the *sense* of the passage. A ship is
supposed to be fighting a tempest, but in the movement of the lines
there isn't even a fresh breeze.

(viii)   Who stooping opened my left side, and took
          From thence a rib, with cordial spirits warm,
          And life-blood streaming fresh; wide was the wound,
          But suddenly with flesh filled up and healed;
          The rib he formed and fashioned with his hands;
          Under his forming hands, a Creature grew,
          Manlike, but different sex, so lovely fair,
          That what seemed fair in all the world, seemed now
          Mean, or in her summed up, in her contained.

In these lines from *Paradise Lost*, Book VIII, Adam is telling the
angel Raphael his dream of God's creation of Eve. The first variation
from strict iambic meter occurs in the third line: *wide was*, a trochee.
This replacement of one foot with another is called S U B S T I T U -
T I O N. And since a trochee is an iamb turned around, we call this
particular substitution an I N V E R S I O N. In this case, the *metrical*
inversion coincides with a *syntactical* inversion. Inversions of either
sort tend to be emphatic because they momentarily startle us, catch
our special attention as something out of the ordinary. Milton might
have written just as easily and in more normal syntax, "the wound was

wide," but Adam naturally wants to emphasize the nature of his wound, perhaps with even a little innocent exaggeration.

Under and *Manlike*, the first feet of lines six and seven respectively, are also inversions, but their main purpose seems to be a rhythmic variation for its own sake. *Mean, or*, the inverted foot in the ninth line, once again underscores the idea of meanness, an effective contrast with the twice-repeated *fair*. Such variations as these keep the verse lively; they provide continual rhythmic variety, and they create subtle emphases.

TROCHAIC

English poets have used trochaic meter principally for very short lyrics and for brief passages of dialogue. There are no long first-rate trochaic poems in English. Perhaps for linguistic and physiological reasons, it seems impossible to sustain an English trochaic poem of any length.

This meter strikes our ear as an unusual kind of beat—more unusual than anapestic, which is like an iamb with an extra nonstress in front. Consequently it seems most appropriate when there is something rather unusual about the subject matter. We find, as a matter of fact, that it is best suited to light and tripping or gnomic and macabre tones, or to a kind of high seriousness that holds an incantatory quality. The trochee, we might say, always jigs or chants:

(*i*)   Foot it featly here and there.

(*ii*)   Swing your partner round and round.

(*iii*)   Jack, be nimble, Jack, be quick.

Those trochaic lines run or dance. When the context is light, as it is there, the novelty of the meter tends to produce a blithely rarefied quality, jigging or speeding effects. But:

(*iv*)   . . . a sea-change
Into something rich and strange.
Sea-nymphs hourly ring his knell.

(v)   Round about the cauldron go;
       In the poisoned entrails throw . . .
       Double, double, toil and trouble;
       Fire burn and cauldron bubble.

(vi)   Weave a circle round him thrice.

Here the qualities of thought and feeling are extraordinary: they
are incantatory, macabre. The unusual meter suits the abnormal
subject.

(vii) Music, when soft voices die,
       Vibrates in the memory;
       Odours, when sweet violets sicken,
       Live within the sense they quicken.

       Rose leaves, when the rose is dead,
       Are heaped for the beloved's bed;
       And so thy thoughts, when thou art gone,
       Love itself shall slumber on.

In the most serious contexts, such as Shelley's stanzas above, trochaic
meter seems appropriate. Opening and usually closing on a stress, it
lends strength to their strong tone, and its unusualness tends to make
the verse memorable.

(viii) Heaping up the shining pebbles,
           Spading in the glistening sand,
       Building fierce but mimic forts
           That from foes shall guard the land,
       Making lovely landscape gardens
           That are watered by the spray,—
               Ah! 'tis surely pleasant
               On the beach to play.

Here there is neither intensity nor a dancing quality. The language
is banal, the handling of the idea tawdry. The meter itself is so
regular as to be wooden (note how Shelley varies his meter in [vii]
by shifting to iambic in the second and third lines of the second stanza).
In short, there is nothing in (viii) to justify the peculiar trochee.

Edgar Allan Poe's famous poem "The Raven," which many people, including the present writers, consider unsuccessful, is written in trochees. In itself, the meter is not unsuited to Poe's melancholy theme and bizarre atmosphere; the poem fails for other reasons—such as its contrived and melodramatic atmosphere and its frequently banal diction and rhyming.

Shakespeare, William Blake, and William Butler Yeats are perhaps the great masters of English trochaic meter.

ANAPESTIC

(*i*)   And the dish ran away with the spoon!

(*ii*)   Sylvia the fair, in the bloom of fifteen,
Felt an innocent warmth as she lay on the green;
She had heard of a pleasure, and something she guessed
By the towzing, and tumbling, and touching her breast.
She saw the men eager, but was at a loss,
What they meant by their sighing, and kissing so close;
    By their praying and whining,
    And clasping and twining,
    And panting and wishing,
    And sighing and kissing,
    And sighing and kissing so close.

We have noticed that the anapest tends to produce lightness and speed. In both of these passages it is a supremely effective meter. The bawdy song stanza is the first of three progressively bawdier ones by John Dryden.

(*iii*)   In an isolated tree a congregation
Of starlings chatter and chide,
Thickset as summer leaves, in garrulous quarrel:
Suddenly they hush as one,—
The tree top springs,—
And off, *with a whirr* of wings,
They fly *by the score.*

The two anapests (indicated by our italics) in the final lines of this passage from Robert Bridges' "November" help suggest the sudden flight of the starlings.

(*iv*)   The hill pines were sighing,
O'ercast and chill was the day:
A mist in the valley lying
Blotted the pleasant May.

But deep in the glen's bosom
Summer slept in the fire
Of the odorous gorse-blossom
And the hot scent of the brier.

A ribald cuckoo clamoured,
And out of the copse the stroke
Of the iron axe that hammered
The iron heart of the oak.

Anon a sound appalling,
As a hundred years of pride
Crashed, in the silence falling:
And the shadowy pine-trees sighed.

The metrical principle of this poem by Bridges is that of three stresses to the line, the stresses falling in no set positions, except on the final syllables of the even-numbered lines (*day:May*), while the odd-numbered lines end on nonstresses (*sighing:lying*). The relative irregularity of the stress pattern makes this a difficult poem to scan. But however one might group the syllables into feet, one thing is apparent: there are several instances of stresses preceded by two nonstresses (*was the day; in the fire*). The effect of these seeming anapests is somewhat obscured by the dominant impression of the regularly repeated, almost randomly spaced, three stresses. In the third stanza, where the theme of the poem begins to become clear, however, we find three anapests coming close on one another's heels, and the effect is distinctly one of speed. But unlike the speed of the Dryden song or in the description of the starlings' flight, it is speed without lightness. What it suggests is rather the quick, relentless strokes of the merciless axe. On occasion, then, anapestic speed may be an urgent or bitter quickening rather than a gay one.

(*v*)   I have gone the whole round of creation; I saw and I spoke:
I, a work of God's hand for that purpose, received in my brain
And pronounced on the rest of his handwork—returned him again
His creation's approval or censure: I spoke as I saw: . . .

Browning's "Saul," a narrative poem of some length, is basically anapestic, and the lines from it quoted above are as perfect a specimen of anapestic pentameter as one will find anywhere. The rhythm does not fit the subject: the movement of the verse has a certain lightness and lilting quality, while the thought and feeling proposed are meditative and sober.

(vi)   Three corpses lay out on the shining sands,
           In the morning gleam, as the tide went down,
        And the women are weeping, and wringing their hands
           For those who will never come home to the town;
              For men must work, and women must weep,
              And the sooner it's over, the sooner to sleep;
              And goodbye to the bar and its moaning.

This last stanza of Charles Kingsley's poem "The Three Fishers" is an even more obvious failure than the Browning lines. The "message" is one of pathos, lamentation, and resignation, but the meter, which is mostly anapestic, makes one almost want to sway with good spirits.

DACTYLIC

Of the four basic meters, dactylic undoubtedly strikes our ear as the most artificial. English poets scarcely tried it at all until the nineteenth century, and now they have all but abandoned it as a meter in its own right.

(i)   Take her up tenderly,
           Lift her with care;
        Fashioned so slenderly,
           Young, and so fair!

This is dactylic dimeter, or two dactyls to a line, alternating with monometer; or, alternately, a dactyl followed by a tailless dactyl. The short passage is far from despicable, but the poem it comes from—Thomas Hood's "The Bridge of Sighs"—continues the dactylic meter for 106 lines, and at that length it becomes, for the reasons we have cited earlier, precious and affected. In serious contexts, the *falling* effect of the dactyl, like that of the trochee, has a tendency to produce an elegiac tone, mournful, wistful, or world-weary. Such a tone is of course suitable for poems like "The Bridge of Sighs" and "Evangeline"; the trouble is that this desirable elegiac quality is embarrassed by the linguistic *unnaturalness* of the English dactyl, and by the *speed* of the recurring pairs of nonstressed sylla-bles. And because a *rising* rhythm (· ⁄ or · · ⁄) seems most indigenous to English ears, the two falling meters—dactylic and trochaic—will tend to be read as anapestic and iambic respectively.

(*ii*)   Little Jack Horner
          Sat in a corner,
          Eating his Christmas pie.

(*iii*)   Leg over leg as the dog went to Dover,
          When he came to a stile, hop! he went over!

(*iv*)   To market, to market, to buy a fat pig;

          Home again, | home again, | jiggety | jig.

These Mother Goose lines are basically, though not purely, dactylic. Prosodists who tell us that the dactyl necessarily makes a somber or melancholy rhythm must have forgotten their nursery days. Once again, the very *oddness* of this foot makes it appropriate to such droll and frisky effects as we find in these children's verses (their prosody is adult enough). Notice too how the speed of the dactyl can be utilized. In (*iii*), where the dog is going at a merry clip, the speed of both trisyllabic feet is exploited: dactylic in the first line, anapestic in the second. The dactyl is probably even better suited to such comic and exuberant effects than to elegiac ones. Linguistic peculiarity and speed are no embarrassment in a light-hearted context.

(*v*)   Hail to the brightness of Zion's glad morning;
              Joy to the lands that in darkness have lain;
          Hushed be the accents of sorrow and mourning;
              Zion in triumph begins her mild reign.

The meter of these lines by Thomas Hastings is as banal as the lan-guage, which is hymnal cliché. The meter is perfectly regular, and such inflexibility is wooden enough in itself; but to make matters worse, this slick, pat, "commercial" rhythm is completely in conflict with the grandeur and masculine strength of the vision. The experience proposed is one of joy and exaltation, but the speed and abnormality of rhyming dactylic meter can result only in hollow and pretty sentiment.

SPONDAIC AND PYRRHIC

I walk | through the | long school | room questioning;

A kind | old nun | in a | white hood | replies; . . .

When stresses occur in succession, meaning almost always demands that some be heavier than others. Consequently, there are few or no true spondees in English verse. But notice in the lines above, from Yeats's "Among School Children," that the stresses on the syllables of the third and fourth feet of the first line, and of the fourth foot of the second line, are more nearly spondees than iambs. It is not really important, however, to be concerned about the *feet*. What is important is to notice that the four consecutive stresses (three primary and one secondary, perhaps) of the first line slow the rhythm to match the sense beautifully. The speaker, an old man who has come as a public official to inspect a school, is walking through a *long* room, and he is moving, of course, unobtrusively and with deliberate care.

In a, the third foot of the second line, is as pure a pyrrhic as one will find in English verse. Notice that the spondee follows immediately. The spondee-pyrrhic or pyrrhic-spondee is one of the commonest variations of iambic meter. Some prosodists prefer to think of the situation as a four-syllable foot called an ıoɴıc. This is a small point.

Notice that the stress on *through* is very light. Compare it with *walk* or *kind*. Should we call *through the* a pyrrhic or a trochee? The final syllable of *questioning* is also extremely light, perhaps lighter than *through*. The constantly varying degree of stress, as we have already noted, is one of the glories of English rhythm; the variation in itself helps prevent monotony in lines otherwise perfectly regular.

5
The Line

Prose moves in units of sentences and paragraphs, poetry in LINES and line groups called STANZAS or sections. In prose, a sentence moves unbrokenly from margin to margin down the page; no typographical break appears until the end of a paragraph. Poetry, on the other hand, shows regular breaks within its sentences. The first sentence of *Paradise Lost* is broken into sixteen lines, of ten syllables each. A single line of verse that forms a complete sentence is rare.

The line is a common feature of all kinds of English poetry: verse and free verse, Anglo-Saxon as well as Modern English poetry. It is, in fact, a nearly universal characteristic of poetry; Greek, Latin, Russian, Chinese, Spanish, Swedish, and Gaelic poetry all move in lines. The only major exceptions to this universality are "prose poetry" and perhaps the Hebrew poetry of Old Testament times. Rhyme, feet, and count of syllables are not nearly so universal; Greek and Roman poetry, for example, did not employ rhyme, and Anglo-Saxon lines show neither rhyme nor count of syllables. The connection, then, between poetry as an art and lining is obviously quite intimate.

45

Many scholars believe that the earliest poetry—no matter where it arose—was chanted or sung. We know that ancient Greek poetry often—and in the beginning almost always—was sung or recited as part of a religious ritual of dance and song. Now syllables and words that must keep time with music or a dance step must accordingly be measured in some way, and for the sake of vocal convenience and ease of memorization these measured units would most naturally be broken into lines.

The line was quite obviously, then, a device for marking the metrical pattern. It was of fundamental importance in keeping the pattern of rhythm from running amuck. Each line break set the typical rhythm going again, regardless of whether the sentence was completed or not. Such a time pattern also acted as an aid to memory, an important consideration for the bard or minstrel who had to memorize thousands of lines. We should also bear in mind that much of the world's ancient poetry was scriptural, and that the division of versified scriptures into lines made it easier to teach by memory. Thus memorability, dramatic emphasis, and the close organization of linguistic detail have tended to make poetry *a structure of lines*.

Keeping in mind that poetry is essentially an oral art intended for recitation in some form, and not for the printed page (despite modern leanings toward the "silent" poem), we can observe something about the line in terms of breathing. We quite naturally desire units of verse that will not leave us breathless. At rest, we draw a breath about every four seconds. An English iambic pentameter line usually consumes no less than two and no more than four seconds. Lines of twelve or more syllables tend to need an internal break:

> As though a rose should shut, and be a bud again;
> ∽
> For if thou diest, my love, I know not where to go.

The average reader would have no difficulty in reading such a twelve-syllable line without drawing a new breath in the middle (after *shut* or *love*), but the pause is convenient and becomes essential as long lines accumulate. In the classical French alexandrine of twelve syllables, a line perhaps more natural to a nonaccentual language, the tendency to pause is greater:

Si je vous aime? O Dieux! mes serments, mes parjures,
Ma fuite, mon retour, mes respects, mes injures . . .

—RACINE

A natural as well as a rhetorical pause (caesura) comes after *Dieux* and after *retour*. Whether the actor delivering these lines would draw a breath at the caesura or not, he would still indicate a pause.

The breathing time of our iambic pentameter, one of the commonest of all poetic lines, is short enough to be convenient and to permit running over into the following line (continual end-stopping would become monotonous), and long enough to provide "working room." Read for example the following sonnet aloud, pausing for breath where you think the expression calls for it. You will probably find that you draw a breath at the beginning of each line except the second:

> How like a winter hath my absence been
> From thee, the pleasure of the fleeting year!
> What freezings have I felt, what dark days seen,
> What old December's bareness every where!
> And yet this time remov'd was summer's time;
> The teeming autumn, big with rich increase,
> Bearing the wanton burthen of the prime,
> Like widowed wombs after their lord's decease:
> Yet this abundant issue seemed to me
> But hope of orphans and unfather'd fruit;
> For summer and his pleasures wait on thee,
> And, thou away, the very birds are mute;
>   Or, if they sing, 'tis with so dull a cheer
>   That leaves look pale, dreading the winter's near.

There are as many as three lines lacking final punctuation of some kind, but most readers would hold their breath only for the first line and a half, which, for rhetorical reasons, cannot wait for a pause. (Throughout his plays, Shakespeare uses a similar device: one speech will end on a half line, and the new speaker will begin by picking up that metrical half:

> *Horatio:*   It was, as I have seen it in his life,
>   A sable silver'd.
> *Hamlet:*   I will watch tonight.)

But with the above exception the sonnet's ten-syllable breath unit is barely disturbed. In dramatic or epic poetry, however, strict regularity is avoided. An actor reciting a Shakespearean passage might hold his breath for two or more full lines.

The decasyllabic line is also suited to our language syntactically. More often than not a line will consist of a clause or clauses, or of nouns or verbs with their modifiers and connectives. Almost half of the lines in the above sonnet, which was chosen at random, might be construed as complete sentences.

Since about ten syllables form a convenient breath unit in English, since our linguistic structures fall so easily into iambic segments, and since our grammar and syntax lend themselves so naturally to conciseness of expression, it is no mystery that iambic pentameter should be our characteristic line. Iambic pentameter and tetrameter have been, in fact, the commonest English meters since the fifteenth century.

And so, although today relatively little poetry of any real merit is written with dancing or recitative in mind, practically all poetry is still written in lines. Emphasis, memorableness, and complete organization of linguistic detail demand a structure of lines. Poets want each syllable to count as much as possible; they want to create a rich and sensitive structure of thought and feeling—

(i)

> Tyger! tyger! burning bright
> In the forests of the night,
> What immortal hand or eye
> Could frame thy fearful symmetry?

The thought of these lines by Blake is no trivial one, and the feeling, that of awesome questioning, is intense. To express such a vision Blake can allow nothing to be casual; he must make his language unusually forceful and vivid. Notice that much of the power and vividness is gained by meter and rhyme. Notice the strength of the trochaic meter. The rhyme not only makes the language more memorable, but also makes the rhyming words, which are key words, more emphatic. This use of meter and rhyme necessarily results in a line structure. Suppose we change Blake's typography to that of ordinary prose:

> Tyger! tyger! burning bright in the forests of the night, what immortal hand or eye could frame thy fearful symmetry?

The rhymes still break the sentence naturally into lines, making the prose typography seem unnatural. But suppose we destroyed the rhymes, substituting unrhyming words for them, and left only the meter? Thus:

> Tyger! tyger! burning fierce in the forests of the night, what immortal eye or hand could frame thy fearful symmetry?

In this case the internal divisions due to sense remain the same, and we still get units that insist on being lines.

(ii)   Beautiful must be the mountains whence ye come,
        And bright in the fruitful valleys the streams wherefrom
            Ye learn your song:
        Where are those starry woods? O might I wander there,
          Among the flowers, which in that heavenly air
            Bloom the year long!

        Nay, barren are those mountains and spent the streams:
        Our song is the voice of desire, that haunts our dreams,
            A throe of the heart,
        Whose pining visions dim, forbidden hopes profound,
          No dying cadence nor long sigh can sound,
            For all our art.

        Alone, aloud in the raptured ear of men
        We pour our dark nocturnal secret; and then,
            As night is withdrawn
        From these sweet-springing meads and bursting boughs of May,
          Dream, while the innumerable choir of day
            Welcome the dawn.

The arrangement of line lengths in Bridges' ode "Nightingales" subtly suggests singing in general and the song of nightingales in particular. The recurring groups of long and very short lines produce the effect of alternating expansion and contraction, and this in turn suggests the varying durations of notes and the varying lengths of melodic lines. Nightingale song is generally a sustained silvery gurgle which closes with a short bar of tones slightly higher in pitch than those of the body. The Elizabethan poet John Lyly represented it like this:

> Jug, Jug, Jug, Jug, Tereu.

With appropriate subtlety Bridges' long lines suggest the body, and the short ones the coda. At the same time, the short lines suggest the brevity of a sigh—in the first stanza, the delicious sighs of the intoxicated listener, in the second and third stanzas, the world-weary, frustrate sighs of the birds themselves.

(*iii*)

> Over the breast of the spring, the land, amid cities,
> Amid lanes and through old woods, where lately the violets peep'd from the ground, spotting the grey debris,
> Amid the grass in the fields each side of the lanes, passing the endless grass,
> Passing the yellow-spear'd wheat, every grain from its shroud in the dark-brown fields uprisen,
> Passing the apple-tree blows of white and pink in the orchards,
> Carrying a corpse to where it shall rest in the grave,
> Night and day journeys a coffin.

Whitman is describing the progress of Abraham Lincoln's funeral train. The very length of these lines suggests the vastness of country and the great length of the journey. The final line is enormously powerful, partly because of its emphatic syntactical structure (notice the inverted word order); partly because it is an epiphany—the point of revelation in a long, suspenseful, periodic sentence; and partly because it is so short a line (eight syllables) that it comes as a kind of shock after the others.

(*iv*)   When lilacs last in the dooryard bloom'd,
> And the great star early droop'd in the western sky in the night,
> I mourned, and yet shall mourn with ever-returning spring.
>
> Ever-returning spring, trinity sure to me you bring,
> Lilac blooming perennial and dropping star in the west,
> And thought of him I love.

The positions of greatest emphasis in a sentence are the end and the beginning, in that order. These same points are emphatic in any unit: phrase, clause, or poetic line. If a sentence, then, is broken into lines, it obtains several additional points of emphasis. For normal prose purposes there is, of course, no reason to do this: so much emphasis and suggestiveness is not appropriate. In (*iv*), the opening section of Whitman's "When Lilacs Last in the Dooryard Bloom'd," some of the words or small word groups that fall at emphatic positions are *lilac(s)*, *bloom'd*, *star*, *night*, *I mourned*, *spring*, *Ever-returning*, and *love*. When we read the whole poem, we discover that these words, as they occur in the opening section, are like first statements of themes in music; later they will be given development, they will be related to one another in an eventually unified context, and they will even become symbols.

(*v*)   Season of mists and mellow fruitfulness,
        Close bosom-friend of the maturing sun:
    Conspiring with him how to load and bless
        With fruit the vines that round the thatch-eves run;
    To bend with apples the mossed cottage-trees,
        And fill all fruit with ripeness to the core;
            To swell the gourd, and plump the hazel shells
    With a sweet kernel; to set budding more,
        And still more, later flowers for the bees,
        Until they think warm days will never cease,
            For Summer has o'er-brimmed their clammy cells.

This is the first stanza of Keats's "To Autumn," a poem that expresses intense but quiet satisfaction, and acceptance of a loving attitude in the face of oncoming decay and death. What part do the lines play in creating an atmosphere of serenity? They are appropriately normal in length, so that the breath does not have to slow down or speed up; they are unusually unbroken by pauses, so that they flow untroubled; and they are all of the same length, so that there is no effect of expansion and contraction to excite placid surface or placid depth.

To sum up, the line is a nearly universal rhetorical feature of poetry. When expression becomes memorably compact, rich, and emphatic, and is highly organized in linguistic detail, lines all but certainly come into being. They provide the poet with a means of obtaining greater control over the medium of words. Through sensitive lining he can obtain and indicate subtle kinds of emphasis; he can suggest in a concrete and plastic way the quality of his subject matter and his attitude toward it. In short, the line provides the greatest possible concentration of meaning and feeling in the most controlled manner possible.

6

Accentual and Syllabic Verse

st,

ng's post.

g heiress,
wood,
s
good,

rise.

keeping the lines decasyllabic)

he warm sun lights up the polished
crimson roses, for her—a service
near it . . .

e that nothing determines the
ning of ten syllables and an
kept the general form of the
at gives the poem its peculiar
elong to prose, but the poem
red.

re, W. H. Auden, Kenneth
-century poets have written
as and Miss Moore usually
ssage from Thomas's "Poem

r-
ees flying my name
rses

ll my days.
I took the road

voke.

Verse that holds to a *fixed number of accents in each line*, but does not fix the position of the accents or the number of unaccented syllables is called ACCENTUAL verse.

Old English poetry was of this type. Here are some lines from *Beowulf:*

Hroðgar maþelode, helm Scyldinga:

"Ic hine cuðe cnihtwesende;

waes his ealdfader Ecgþeo haten."

(Then Hrothgar, the Scylding king, spoke up:
"I know him, I know him, knew him as a boy,
And I knew his father, old Edgethow.")

Coleridge, Hopkins, Eliot, and many other poets have experimented, sometimes quite successfully, with accentual verse. Here

is a short accentual poem by Hopkins which, like the
fixes four stresses to a line:

> *At the Wedding March*
> God with honour hang your head,
> Groom, and grace you, bride, your **bed**
> With lissome scions, sweet scions,
> Out of hallowed bodies bred.
>
> Each be other's comfort kind:
> Déep, déeper than divined,
> Divine charity, dear charity,
> Fast you ever, fast bind.
>
> Then let the march tread our ears:
> I to him turn with tears
> Who to wedlock, his wonder wedlock,
> Déals tríumph and immortal years.

T. S. Eliot has used accentual verse successfully;
from the second section of "Ash Wednesday," sh
stresses in each line, and an indeterminate num
syllables:

> Lá"> Lády of sílences
>
> Cálm and distréssed
>
> Tórn and most whóle
>
> Róse of mémory
>
> Róse of forgétfulness
>
> Exháusted and lífe-giving
>
> Wórried repóseful.

Verse that merely *counts the number of*
and neither counts the stresses nor distributes
is known as SYLLABIC verse. In a syllabic
language in which stress is weak or nonexistent–
of verse to construct. French verse is traditio

> rolls in a napkin, fairy rack of toa
> butter in ice, high silver coffee-po
> and, heaped on a salver, the morni
>
> She comes over the lawn, the your
> from her early walk in her garden
> feeling that life's a table set to ble
> her delicate desires with all that's
>
> that even the unopened future lies
> like a love-letter, full of sweet sur

Suppose we change the rhyme words (
and then write the sonnet as prose:

> Through the open French window t
> breakfast-table, laid round a bowl o
> of Worcester porcelain, and placed

With the rhyme out of the way, we s
prosody of the poem except the assig
end rhyme to every line. The poet has
sonnet, but it is the absence of meter th
character. The rhythms of the poem b
is not prosaic, and has been much admi

Dylan Thomas, Marianne Mo
Rexroth, and several other twentieth
syllabic verse of high quality. Thom
employ rhyming syllabics. Here is a p
in October":

> My birthday began with the wat
> Birds and the birds of the winged tr
> Above the farms and the white h
> And I rose
> In rainy autumn
> And walked abroad in a shower of
> High tide and the heron dived when
> Over the border
> And the gates
> Of the town closed as the town a

A springful of larks in a rolling
Cloud and the roadside bushes brimming with whistling
Blackbirds and the sun of October
  Summery
  On the hill's shoulder,
Here were fond climates and sweet singers suddenly
Come in the morning where I wandered and listened
  To the rain-wringing
  Wind blow cold
In the wood faraway under me.

Symmetry is the principle here. Each line in a stanza has the same number of syllables as the corresponding line of succeeding stanzas. Where more than one line in the same stanza has the same number of syllables, Thomas gives them the same typographical indentation. For instance, the first and last lines of each stanza have nine syllables and the same indentation. The syllable count by lines runs as follows: 9, 12, 9, 3, 5, 12, 12, 5, 3, 9. There is also rhyme in the stanzas (the uninitiated will not detect it), strong but irregular alliteration, and strong but irregularly placed metrical groups (as in *sún of Octóber*, *fáráway únder me, brímming with whístling*). Still the chief prosodic principle is the count of syllables.

Marianne Moore has been more consistently a syllabic prosodist than most other English or American poets, and has experimented with widely varying line lengths and with rhyme, as in her famous poem "The Fish":

The Fish
wade
through black jade
  Of the crow-blue mussel-shells, one
   keeps
   adjusting the ash heaps;
    opening and shutting itself like
an
injured fan.
  The barnacles which encrust the side
  of the wave, cannot hide
  there for the submerged shafts of
   the . . . '

The novelty and cleverness of her metric are consonant with the freshness and wit so characteristic of this poet's perceptions, and the kinetic quality of the expanding and contracting lines seems especially appropriate to her favorite subject—animals in action.

All these writers show some degree of dissatisfaction with the traditional stress-pattern prosody of English poetry, and they attempt to meet the requirements of contemporary diction and informal speech structures. But there is little likelihood that syllabic prosody will ever displace more determinate systems. The limitations of syllable-counting as a basis of English meter are obvious, and nearly all syllabists feel it necessary to add rhyme or typographical spacing as a buttress.

Our native meter was *accentual:*

$$
\begin{array}{cccc}
/ & / & / & / \\
\end{array}
$$
Oft Scyld Scefing   sceaþena þreatum,

$$
\begin{array}{cccc}
/ & / & / & / \\
\end{array}
$$
monegum maegþum   meodosetla ofteah.

Measuring verse by counting the strong stresses was an ineradicable habit by the time of the Norman invasion (1066).

But of course a powerful French linguistic influence began immediately. The Normans measured their verse by syllable count and end rhyme:

1   2   3   4   5   6   78
Or vous ert par ce livre apris,

1   2   3 4   5 6 78
Que Gresse or de chevalerie

1   2   3 4 5 6 7   8
Le premier los et de clergie.

(Now by this book you will learn
that Greece first had the renown
for chivalry and letters.)

A process of compromise between the accentual and the syllabic modes set in at once. Englishmen agreed to count the number of syllables, but insisted on continuing to count the number of accents too. The result is the accentual-syllabic line, first used as the medium of great English poetry by Chaucer:

> Now | have | I | told | you | short |ly, | in | a | clau|se,|
> 1   2   3   4   5   6   7   8   9   10 11
>
> Th' es|tat, | th' ar|ray, | the | nombre, | and | eek | the | caus|e,
> 1   2   3   4   5   6   7   8   9   10 11
>
> Why that assembled was this compan-y-e
> 1   2   3 4   5   6   7   8   9 10 11
>
> In Southwerk, at this gentil hostel-ry-e.
> 1   2   3   4 5   6   7   8 9 10 11

Historically, there has been a tendency to observe the syllable count more strictly than the count of accents. Pentameter lines of only three or four strong stresses are quite common, but in a sense the places of the missing stresses are filled by those of the ideal or theoretical five-stress pattern, which runs in our head and even influences our reading. Notice that of the four lines above, only the second corresponds to the theoretical pattern.

This evolution of our now traditional accentual-syllabic line was virtually uninfluenced by the "foot" system. The poets themselves, almost to a man, were getting their consciousness of language and their inspiration from native English (accentual) and the newly fashionable French (syllabic) sources, not from Latin or Greek quantitative verse and its "foot thinking."

7
Meter and Rhythm

Although the words METER and RHYTHM are often used synonymously, it is useful to maintain a distinction between them. In speaking of verse, we ought to say, "This *meter* is iambic," not "this *rhythm*." Rhythm is *the total quality of a line's motion*, and is a product of several elements, not of stress or of quantity alone.

Probably no two lines of poetry, and no two sentences of prose, have exactly the same rhythm, although the difference is often so slight as to be of no consequence. In a Shakespeare sonnet, each of the fourteen lines is iambic pentameter, but each has a rhythm peculiar to itself; in some cases, the differences may be very great.

Meter in itself—although not in its functions—is a relatively simple matter that we can usually describe with great objectivity. Rhythm is always complex and is often difficult to describe. Meter is a matter of mechanics; rhythm is almost unanalyzably organic. There are, at least in English, relatively few possible meters, whereas every new combination of words really brings about a new rhythm:

Since brass, nor stone, nor earth, nor boundless sea,

But sad mortality o'ersways their power . . .

Both of these lines are iambic pentameter (each has ten syllables, the even-numbered ones being stressed), but each line has a rhythm all its own. The first is slow, deliberate, grave. The second moves much more quickly, and it moves as a whole—whereas the first line gives the effect of a number of distinct parts moving together. It is obvious at a glance that much of the rhythmical difference in these two lines is accounted for by the fact that the first, unlike the second, is broken into a series of units. But many other differences contribute to the difference in rhythm. For example, the fact that the first line is made up almost entirely of monosyllables, and the fact that the second line shows a pause, at the end of the sixth syllable, which breaks the syntax into two nearly equal members: *But sad mortality*—subject; *o'ersways their power*—predicate. Note too that a word of two or more syllables always tries to preserve its integrity, so that in these two lines, as in most others, there is a pleasing conflict (or counterpoint or tension) between the regular pull of the meter and the varying pull of the individual words themselves, their lexical stresses. And of course this conflict itself will vary from line to line, as the words themselves change. Thus, while the first line is regular iambic, the word *boundless* refuses to be torn in two by the meter. We have then toward the end of the line, playing against the metrical rhythm, what we might call the P H R A S A L rhythm:

> Since brass, | nor stone, | nor earth, | nor boundless | sea.

Another example of this counterpoint between word, or phrase, and meter is the line:

> And of|ten is | his gold | complex|ion dimm'd.

The phrasal rhythm—determined by meaning, idiom, and word integrity—is something like this:

> And often | is his gold | complexion dimm'd.

Let us take still another example which shows that stress, however important in determining the rhythmic structure of verse, is only one of several elements that when brought together result in the quality of motion we call rhythm.

Here are two more lines of perfectly regular iambic meter;
in various ways—phrasing and tone or level of intensity, for example
—they are much more nearly alike than the two lines of our first
example:

To roll the torrent out of dusky doors,

Their thousand wreaths of dangling watersmoke.

For all their similarity, however, the two lines are utterly unlike in
rhythm. The first line runs by with an effect of straightforward speed;
the second is slow and circuitous like its own image. One reason for
the second line's reluctant, coiling effect is its numerous relatively
effortful and time-consuming diphthongs, long vowels, and resonant
syllables. Here, then, we see how *quantity* and *color* may be as important as stress in determining rhythm. And of course *meaning* itself
is of great importance. In fact, it is impossible really to perceive
the rhythm of a line until we can make some kind of sense of it.
Meaning has relatively little control over the sound or quantity of
a syllable, but it directs among other things the pausing, the rise and
fall of pitch, and to some extent the degree of stress on the individual
syllable. It is easy to demonstrate that no matter what the mechanics
of a line—no matter what collocations of sounds, stresses, and quantities we may find—the line will seem to move faster if the meaning
or image has to do with speed or high excitement, and more slowly
if it expresses, let us say, heartbreak or drowsiness. Thus, in the
langorous, narcotic setting of Tennyson's poem "The Lotos-Eaters,"
lines such as

The charmèd sunset lingered low adown

or

To watch the long bright river drawing slowly

seem even slower than they are intrinsically. Compare Byron's line,

The Assyrian came down like the wolf on the fold

with Poe's,

For the moon never beams without bringing me dreams.

Although both of these last lines are anapestic tetrameter, the second has not nearly the first's speed. Poe's line contains considerably more pace-slowing resonance than Byron's, but another reason for its relative slowness is the fact that its sense simply calls for a moderate tempo, whereas Byron's line urges us to match vocally the speed of its image.

Stress, then, is a powerful element in the rhythm of English verse. We saw earlier, for example, how in a sequence of lines a metronomic regularity in the stress pattern tends to override other rhythmic elements and produce a monotonous cadence. But stress is only one of several things that contribute to the total quality of a line's movement.

Meter should be defined as the theoretically regular, although in practice sometimes much varied, recurring pattern of acoustic detail within the line. In modern English verse the pattern consists of a fixed number of stresses and of fixed positions for them in relation to the unstressed, or more lightly stressed, syllables. The mere ordered physical placement of stresses and nonstresses tends to create a determinate acoustic structure—that is, to convey a sense of regularity or symmetry—and this structure is enhanced by the ISOCHRONIC principle, the fact that the intervals between primary stresses tend to seem equal. In Old English poetry, only the number of stresses per line was fixed; in French poetry the number of syllables and the end rhymes are the determinants; in Greek and Latin poetry the numbers of long and short syllables and their positions were the fixed elements; in Chinese poetry the principle is that of variation in pitch together with a fixed count of syllables. Thus, for a definition that will cover all instances, we have to describe METER as the distribution of syllables according to stress, quantity, pitch, or mere number, in some regular pattern either within the line or among successive lines.

When we designate the meter of a stanza or poem, it is customary to indicate also the number of metrical units or feet in each line. A line of only one foot gives us MONOMETER; of two feet, DIMETER; of five, PENTAMETER; of seven, HEPTAMETER, etc.

As we have defined it, meter is only one of the several elements that go to make up verse rhythm. If we try to identify meter or mere stress itself with rhythm—a traditional misconception of the matter—we would have to conclude that prose and free verse, since they are without meter, are also without rhythm; an obvious absurdity. It would seem that to hold a true conception of rhythm, we must forsake all hope of a neat and precise analysis. We may not perhaps safely go beyond the idea that rhythm is *the overall quality of movement we feel* in a line or sentence or paragraph or larger unit, and that it is almost infinitely variable. We might compare rhythm to a river: its tributaries are such things as stress, duration of syllables, pauses, phrasing or syntax, and overall meaning. And like a river, any rhythm is full of intricate, almost unanalyzable currents, and is constantly changing its pace and mood.

Rhythm has traditionally been identified with *regularity*, but this seems to be an oversimplification we must learn to do without. As a matter of fact, we are tempted to call *un*rhythmical a succession of lines in which the meter is too regular! Of many passages in Gifford's translation of Juvenal, we are likely to say, "stiff, wooden, not rhythmical."

The following two lines show great regularity, both in themselves and as compared with each other:

> Music, when soft voices die . . .
> Rose leaves, when the rose is dead.

Certainly no one has ever hesitated to call these lines rhythmical; but consider this line:

> Cover her face: mine eyes dazzle: she died young.

The rhythm is impressive, moving, even apart from context. But where is the regularity?

It is true enough that we easily find pleasure in a verse rhythm that shows a good deal of regularity in its meter; but if we look at poetry itself rather than at theories, in the right contexts a beat of

> ONE two | ONE two three | one TWO | one two THREE |
> ONE TWO

can seem as "rhythmical" as a beat of

> ONE two | ONE two | ONE two three | ONE two three.

We find such "irregular" rhythms everywhere—in prose, in free and syllabic verse, and in music from Stravinsky to the present. Wherever there is movement, there is rhythm. It may be as metronomically regular as the beat of the heart, or as varying as the movement of ordinary prose. It is fruitless to argue—as some prosodists have argued profitlessly for many years now—over what is the real basis of English rhythm. We have to rely on our own aesthetic responses to a line. We perceive the movement, and we can usually find adjectives that roughly describe it—"regular and dignified," "rapid and broken," "breathless," "lax." We know that the syllables in any line or sentence have such qualities as stress and quantity; we know that meaning and syntax are changing from point to point; and we know finally that all these things coalesce into a certain unique quality of motion. If we define rhythm in this way, then the search for some *one* determinant of English rhythm proves to be, as we think it is, the pursuit of the chimera.

All this does not mean that an expression such as, "This is rhythmical," has no meaning or must be abandoned in ordinary conversation. We need only remember, in order to avoid the mistake of identifying meter with rhythm or rhythm with regularity of sequence, that when we make such a remark we really mean one or both of two things: (1) that we perceive a high degree of *regularity* in the movement; (2) that we are *pleased* by the movement, whether it be in fact regular or irregular.

When the movement of lines of poetry fails to avoid monotony or is inappropriate to their tone or meaning, we have unsatisfactory rhythm—but a rhythm exists, nonetheless. *Unrhythmical* can logically mean only unsatisfactory rhythm.

Finally, it is interesting to note that our language has what amounts to a built-in protection against monotony of rhythm, so that long stretches of wooden rhythm are really quite rare. Because rhythm is bound to change as the words and syntax change, perfect regularity is not only undesirable, it is almost impossible. Often, when we say that we don't like a poem because its rhythm is monotonous, close inspection will show that the trouble arises more from rhetorical vices such as redundancy, diffuseness, weak diction, poor word placement, and so forth, than from rhythmic ineptitude.

8

The Uses of Meter

Meter is ancient and persistent. It had vigor for Homer and Hesiod three thousand years ago, and it has had vigor for modern poets like Dylan Thomas and Robert Frost. Prose and free verse have come alongside it, but have not replaced it or made it obsolete in any sense. Even free verse—as many poets, critics, and scholars have pointed out—is usually much closer to formal, metrical poetry than it is to prose. Here, for example, is the opening of Wallace Stevens' poem "Domination of Black":

> At night, by the fire,
> The colors of the bushes
> And of the fallen leaves,
> Repeating themselves,
> Turned in the room,
> Like the leaves themselves
> Turning in the wind.

Notice that Stevens exploits the principle of the line as thoroughly as he would do in an orthodox metrical poem. The short lines serve to give great emphasis to each image and each phase of thought, and to slow down the poem's tempo. Notice too that each line contains exactly two strong stresses. And notice the unprosaic repetitions: *The colors . . . repeating themselves . . . turned . . . the fallen leaves . . . like the leaves themselves . . . turned . . . turning.* The passage is not at all like prose, nor would it seem any more like it even if we were to present it as such typographically.

Stevens' lines resemble accentual verse. In the free verse of Walt Whitman we often find all the characteristics of ordinary metrical verse, especially a tendency for the lines to fall into a loose—and occasionally a very regular—iambic meter. Here are the first two sections of "When Lilacs Last in the Dooryard Bloom'd":

1
When lilacs last in the dooryard bloom'd,
And the great star early droop'd in the western sky in the night,
I mourn'd, and yet shall mourn with ever-returning spring.

Ever-returning spring, trinity sure to me you bring,
Lilac blooming perennial and drooping star in the west,
And thought of him I love.

2
O powerful western fallen star!
O shades of night—O moody, tearful night!
O great star disappear'd—O the black murk that hides the star!
O cruel hands that hold me powerless—O helpless soul of me!
O harsh surrounding cloud that will not free my soul.

Notice the numerous instances of *inverted word order* (a device usually associated with formal verse) in the first section. And the *assonance* and *internal rhyming: bloom'd . . . droop'd . . . returning . . . spring . . . bring . . . blooming . . . drooping.* Finally, the whole passage scans as iambic meter; in fact, all the lines except two and five are fairly regular, some almost perfectly so:

Ever- | return | ing spring, | trinit | y sure | to me | you bring . . .

O harsh | surround | ing cloud | that will | not free | my soul.

Obviously poetry is congenial to meter, and vice versa. Individual poets and theorists have usually identified this congeniality with the one or two aspects of meter that struck them most forcibly in their own experience. David Hume and Wordsworth, for example, stressed meter's power to give pleasure as a time pattern, and according to Wordsworth to temper "the painful feeling always found intermingled with powerful descriptions of the deeper passions." Yeats emphasized the hypnotic and suggestive powers of meter; and William Temple, Archbishop of York, thought that its primary function was to catch and hold the reader's attention, as a frame helps focus our attention on the picture it encloses, and prevent the eye from wandering. There is truth, but not anything like the whole truth, in each of these ideas. Actually meter does a great deal of work in verse, and accomplishes its tasks in various ways. Or, if one prefers to look at it from the opposite angle, there are a great many things about the way language is used in poetry that invite the formal disposition of stresses we call meter. To explore the several functions of meter, then, is to explore at the same time poetry as poetry. Our own exploration in this chapter is phrased in terms of the orthodox metrical verse—that is, accentual-syllabic verse—that has been the dominant form from Wyatt and Surrey to the present.

I.   THE EXPRESSION OF FEELING

Poetry always expresses feeling of one kind or another. Emotion and attitude, along with perception and imagination, are the very heart of poetry. Often the emotion we find in the great and good poetry of the past is very strong. Emotional intensity is especially characteristic of L Y R I C poetry—the kind of poetry that has evolved especially for the expression of powerful feeling. But other kinds of poetry too—narrative, dramatic, reflective—can show strong imagination and feeling. Now we have long known that when we try to express intense feeling of any kind, our language tends to become more regular. We repeat ourselves, in order to gain emphasis; energy and attention are fixed on whatever it is that induces the strong feeling. Notice the quasi-metrical quality of Ruth's famous appeal to Naomi:

> Intreat me not to leave thee, or to return
> from following after thee: for whither thou goest,
> I will go; and where thou lodgest, I will lodge:
> thy people shall be my people, and thy God my God.

Regularity has come into the expression as *parallelism* and *repetition*. In the same way, the regularity of *meter* can seem expressive of strong feeling. When Shakespeare's Cleopatra says, in strictest meter,

> Give me my robe, put on my crown. I have
> Immortal longings in me,

we feel that the meter somehow makes the emotion more vivid and moving.

And the *pleasure* meter creates—the purely formal pleasure, apart from context—may heighten the emotional quality of a passage. Fulke Greville begins a poem,

> You little stars that live in skies,

and we feel the mere pleasure of the meter sweetening and coloring a line whose conceptual impact does not seem to amount to much.

But the matter is not so simple. Meter is paradoxical. It tends to *modify* emotion at the same time as it seems to express it. Meter seems appropriate to emotional and imaginative expression not only because it suggests and stimulates feeling, but also because it makes the language in which it appears unlike the language (and experiences) of everyday. Meter introduces a note of the consciously planned, the symmetrical and artful, and thus makes our experience of reading verse an experience greatly different from our direct involvement in ordinary discourse and from our participation in an actual emotional situation. In other words, meter can be a means of obtaining what is often called "aesthetic distance" or "psychic distance."

Considered in itself, a regular beat—whether it be a drum beat, a rhythmical stamping of feet, or an iambic pentameter—evokes and seems to express strong feeling. It unquestionably has connections with the primitive, the emotional, the instinctual, aspects of our nature. In verse, however, meter does not exist independently, but in a context of words; it is conjoined with images and ideas, with a grammar and a rhetoric. And since the determinateness of the beat is "artificial"—a formality, an artifice, a quality not characteristic of ordinary discourse—meter tends to *remove* poetic discourse from the realm of the ordinary. It creates an aura of distance and indirectness and yields all the pleasures that we derive from such a remove from the direct and the familiar. It satisfies our love of formality, ritual, detachment. Simultaneously, the note of urgency, the hint of the primitive or of intense response, is never quite lost. Metered poetry thus makes a simultaneous appeal to two distinct sides of the personality, and this no doubt is one reason for the continuing appeal of meter from generation to generation and age to age. It is a paradigm of civilization: Bacchus dancing with Athena.

Aesthetic distance is what softens the blow of calamity. It is what keeps us from *completely* accepting the calamities in *King Lear* as real-life calamities happening before our very eyes, so that we do not rush out of our seats to knock Cornwall down when he starts to stamp out poor old Gloucester's eyes. In real life, sorrow makes us feel sorrowful; on the stage, or in a great lyric poem, the expression of joy or serenity or sublimity can bring tears. In a Shakespeare play we project ourselves imaginatively into the unfolding situation and its characters—but never completely forget that what we are seeing is an illusion, a re-creation, and not a real situation. What keeps us in this back-of-the-mind awareness? First of all, active memory, of course. And the marginal consciousness of the theatre and the rest of the audience. But there is something about a Shakespeare play itself that creates aesthetic distance. For one thing, our faint but never quite extinguished sense of the unreality, the impossibility, of such eloquence and synchrony for real people in a real situation. For another, all those aspects of the play that are deliberately symbolic and nonrepresentational, rather than realistic, such as condensed time, and the cutting out of the lags and redundancies and inexpressive locutions inevitable in everyday conversation and behavior. And for another, the meter, the *blank verse*. Meter—even the normally loose meter of dramatic blank verse—is just artificial (or studied or formal) enough to keep in the realm of poetry the relentless torture and suffering and defeat of the good in *Lear*.

The classic expressions of this particular function of aesthetic distance are by Wordsworth and Hume. In the famous Preface to *Lyrical Ballads*, Wordsworth pointed out that because of

> the tendency of meter to divest language, in a certain degree, of its reality, and thus to throw a sort of half-consciousness of insubstantial existence over the whole composition, there can be little

doubt but that more pathetic situations and sentiments, that is, those which have a greater proportion of pain connected with them, may be endured in metrical composition, especially in rhyme, than in prose.

And in his essay "Of Tragedy" Hume observed that

> The force of imagination, the energy of expression, the power of numbers [i. e., meter] . . . are . . . delightful to the mind. The passion, though perhaps naturally, and when excited by the simple appearance of a real object, it may be painful; yet is so smoothed and softened, and mollified, when raised by the finer arts, that it affords the highest entertainment.

The mystery, the paradox, remains: meter seems both to express and to chasten emotion at the same time. Art is at least as complex as life.

II.   FORMALISM

The first minute or so of *King Lear* is far from intense. The characters show no particular depth of feeling, nor any incisiveness of perception. Kent and Gloucester, two noblemen waiting in Lear's palace, begin to talk. At first they speak casually about the king's attitude toward two other noblemen, the Dukes of Albany and Cornwall. Then Kent notices Gloucester's "natural" son Edmund standing nearby, and speaks with him politely and congenially until the king enters. All this is in prose. But then Lear enters, and facing the assembled company, begins:

> Meantime we shall express our darker purpose.
> Give me the map there. Know that we have divided
> In three our kingdom; and 'tis our fast intent
> To shake all cares and business from our age,
> Conferring them on younger strengths while we
> Unburthened crawl toward death.

Lear is announcing his intentions before an audience of family and courtiers. This is a formal situation, and in fact Lear, out of vanity, wants everything to appear even more formal and ceremonious than

the situation demands—and reason would recommend. The same
pattern holds throughout the play: as a situation becomes more
formal, the language tends toward verse.

Whatever else verse is, it is a highly formal use of language:
its organization is thorough and unordinary—words and syllables
are placed according to sound and stress and connotative value;
immediately clear and straightforward sense is not, as it normally is
in prose, the highest value. A formal tone and a formal human situation
find a natural complement in the formal structure of verse. Arthur
Miller in his essay "The Family in Modern Drama" points out that
we tend to become formal when we face anyone outside the circle of
our own family and very closest friends—when we face society, in
short. We become self-protective, and at the same time we try to
put the best foot forward, in language as in other things. This tendency toward formality thus turns our ordinary language—the intimate, colloquial kind of language we use within the family and in
circles of friends—in the direction of poetry. Poetry has been described
as man's best thoughts in the best language. When we begin to purge
our expressions of their ordinary vices—lax rhythms, trite figures,
weak abstractions, hesitations, and redundancies—when we do this
in order to communicate with real vigor and persuasiveness, we are
moving toward poetry and ultimately, of course, toward verse.

Meter, then, formalizes, or tends to formalize, language; and
poetry lies in the direction of the selective and the formal, rather
than in the direction of the casual and loosely disciplined.

III.   ENGAGING INTEREST

The speech of characters in a play—tragedy or comedy,
O'Neill or Shakespeare—is almost always a good deal more interesting than the little-rehearsed speech of everyday life. That's one
reason we go to the theatre: we've had enough of the everyday, and
want now to see and hear something superior, more lively, more
meaningful. On the stage, or on the screen, faithful transcription
of actual dialogue bores us—theatre-laboratory experiments have
demonstrated this. The playwright whose plays will endure is
constantly *selecting* from a mass of possible action and possible
dialogue. He selects what clarifies or strengthens his theme, his

vision of life, and he discards the rest. The novelist and the poet do the same. Language must be constructed so that it will gain and continually maintain our attention. Verse—and of course nonmetrical poetry as well—catches and holds our interest because it is not the usual thing, and because it is more than usually efficient and pleasing. Hence another very obvious but very important function of meter is its immediate power to engage us, to make curious readers or listeners out of us. Right away we feel that a person who speaks to us in such an unusual way must have some novel or unusually deep and rich attitude or experience to communicate.

IV. SENSUOUS VIVIDNESS

Meter has the peculiar power to create in us a heightened awareness of the meanings of words themselves.

If we compare our reading of verse with our reading of ordinary expository prose, we find that in verse each word seems more sensuous, and to have more of a life of its own. Reading a sentence, we race along in pursuit of the idea, the intellectual substance. We are certainly aware too of *how* a thing is being said in prose, but the information or opinion or illustration or step in logic is the immediate, the supremely important aim, and we find ourselves hurrying to grasp it. But poetry, although it also deals or may deal with information, opinion, and even logical analysis, always aims to present its experience in such a way that the reader—and the poet who writes the poem is the first reader—can re-create vividly in his own imagination the situation and the qualities of feeling the poem presents. In T. E. Hulme's phrase, poetry often tries to "hand over sensations bodily" and prevent our "gliding through an abstract process." Now there are all sorts of ways of obtaining the vividness and forcefulness we desire in poetry—especially in lyric poetry. Concrete diction, rhythm and sound that in some way suggest or complement the sense, and fresh metaphor are a few of those ways. Meter itself is another.

It is easier to assent to this idea, however, than to explain just how it is that setting words in such an order that there is a fairly predictable pattern of stresses and nonstresses makes the words themselves more sensuous, more like tangible *things*, and in some way *fresher* than we ordinarily find them. The *sensitivity* to connotation and to qualities of sound and rhythm that poetry creates in us and demands of us as we read probably carries over to our apprehension of the individual words. And the mere fact that we find syllables distributed in an abnormal pattern probably makes us unusually sensitive to the words they make up. In any event, it is more important to be aware of this sensory function of meter than to be able to account for it precisely.

(i)   Th' expense of spirit in a waste of shame
        Is lust in action; and till action, lust
        Is perjur'd, murd'rous, bloody, full of blame,
        Savage, extreme, rude, cruel, not to trust;
        Enjoy'd no sooner but despised straight;
        Past reason hunted, and no sooner had,
        Past reason hated, as a swallowed bait
        On purpose laid to make the taker mad;
        Mad in pursuit, and in possession so;
        Had, having, and in quest to have, extreme;
        A bliss in proof—and prov'd, a very woe;
        Before, a joy propos'd; behind, a dream.
            All this the world well knows; yet none knows well
            To shun the heaven that leads men to this hell.

Notice that the diction in this poem runs counter to what we expect in lyrics: it is remarkably abstract. The poem is all but totally devoid of even the most elementary imagery. And yet it is a successful poem. For its imaginative impact, it depends a great deal on meter and rhythm. There is strong and almost continual conflict between the iambic meter and the phrasal rhythm; the phrasing itself is choppy, and the individual words become enormously emphatic. A free verse poem made up of such successions of generic and abstract words is almost unthinkable.

V.   UNITY AND VARIATION

We delight in form, order, regularity, predictability: we stipulate only that these things not become monotonous, that they be enlivened by some irregularities here and there. So powerful is our fear of uncertainty and chaos that we sometimes overinsist upon order, to the point of ennui in sensibility, and of fallacy in thought and perception. In Bacon's words, "The human understanding is of its own nature prone to suppose the existence of more order and regularity in the world than it finds."

We also delight in perceiving unity in variety—in a balance or tension between something fixed and something changing. In a baroque design, for example, we may be fascinated by a network of interlacing curves: the shapes and sizes of the curves and enclosed spaces vary, but the principle of the curve remains constant, and the figures will be juxtaposed symmetrically. In a Bach fugue the same motif appears again and again, but in different voices, in notes of different value, or in inverted order.

These two principles, though similar, are really distinct: the one implies a love of symmetry, of exact repetition for its own sake; the other a love of contrasts held together in harmony. In any successful verse, we are attracted by the regularity of the meter and by its contrast with the continual changes in all the other elements—sounds, quantities, pauses, and so forth.

Notice the metrical structure of these lines from a magnificent speech by Prospero in *The Tempest:*

> Our revels now are ended. These our actors,
> As I foretold you, were all spirits and
> Are melted into air, into thin air.

The verse, iambic pentameter, is almost, though not quite, perfectly regular: the basic metrical unit—the iambic foot—is counterpointed by other elements that make up the rhythm. There is a sweet struggle going on. The first two feet are *Our rev|els now*, but we *read* this phrase as *Our revels | now*. The meter has no chance to become mechanical.

Shakespeare has avoided what is known as DIAERESIS, which comes about when the beginning or end of a *foot* coincides with the beginning or end of a *word*. Ordinarily, continued diaeresis is to be avoided, as it tends to make a line seem mechanical and inharmonious. It breaks the line into detached parts and it makes the stresses seem monotonously equal in force. Notice how Gifford, in these lines from his translation of Juvenal, has created monotony by consistently allowing diaeresis:

> And now | for nymphs | we call, | and now | for wine.
> And have | I wreaked | on such | foul deeds | my rage,
> That worse | should yet | remain | to blot | my page.

The trick is to allow some of the feet within a line to begin and end in the middle of a word, as they do in *Our revels now are ended*. This allows the feet to be more closely, and thus more smoothly, linked together. Notice, though, that like most rules, the avoidance of diaeresis has its exceptions. In the Shakespeare sonnet beginning "The' expense of spirit in a waste of shame," both lines of the closing couplet violate the principle (the twelfth line too shows diaeresis, but punctuation mitigates the mechanical effect). However, the effect here seems to be intentional; in Gifford's lines it seems to be mere incompetence or carelessness. Shakespeare's couplet is intended to stand in strong contrast to what has come before, and it is intended to be rhythmically somewhat flat and dry: the wrath and anxiety are over, and rational incisiveness, irony, and a half-amused disenchantment with human nature have set in. In any event, because of the preponderance of English monosyllables, stretches of diaeresis are difficult to avoid, and our ear seems to have grown rather tolerant of them.

VI. VARIATION FOR EMPHASIS

Meter establishes a convention, a normal pattern, in which variations may take on significance. The principle depends on the psychology of contrast and surprise: we immediately notice pronounced irregularities in the midst of a surrounding regularity, and these irregularities seem emphatic because they catch our attention so forcibly. Metrical variations frequently exist for their own sake, of course: they are necessary if the meter itself is not to become monotonous. But as we noted earlier, they may also be used to emphasize an idea or image at the point where they occur, and to indicate changes in tone. Some additional illustrations may prove helpful.

Earth has not anything to show more fair;
Dull would he be of soul who could pass by
A sight so touching in its majesty:
This City now doth, like a garment, wear
The beauty of the morning.

This is the opening of a Wordsworth sonnet. Its very first foot is a trochaic substitution, and so is the first foot of the second line. Now there is no need for variation for the sake of relief so early in the meter. The trochees obviously function to throw emphasis upon *Earth* and *Dull*. The whole point of the two lines is that nowhere else *on earth* is there a sight more impressive, and that only an *extraordinary dullness* could fail to become aware of it.

It is a beauteous evening, calm and free;
The holy time is quiet as a nun
Breathless with adoration; the broad sun
Is sinking down in its tranquility;
The gentleness of heaven broods o'er the sea:
Listen! the mighty Being is awake,
And doth with his eternal motion make
A sound like thunder—everlastingly.
Dear child! dear girl! that walkest with me here,
If thou appear untouched by solemn thought,
Thy nature is not therefore less divine:
Thou liest in Abraham's bosom all the year,
And worship'st at the Temple's inner shrine,
God being with thee when we know it not.

Notice the ninth line of this sonnet: at this point there is a sudden increase in excitement, and the meter responds accordingly. The tone of the first eight lines is one of reverence and wonder. Then the speaker's attention turns lovingly and almost rapturously to the young girl; it is her winning human presence and his own wonder at the state of grace he imagines her to be in that quicken his feeling so powerfully. Now the iambic meter of the first eight lines seems particularly quiet, and we find in most of them a metrical peculiarity: seldom are there five strong stresses in a line. In most of the lines there are four primary stresses and one secondary stress, and the fourth line contains only three stresses of good force:

Is sinking down in its tranquility.

But the high-pitched ninth line scans like this:

Dear child! dear girl! that walkest with me here.

Only two of the ten syllables may be said to be unstressed. The strength of stress carries the strength of feeling.

Robert Bridges' "Eros" is written in iambic tetrameter couplets. In it the speaker faces and comments upon a statue or painting of the Greek god:

> Why hast thou nothing in thy face?
> Thou idol of the human race,
> Thou tyrant of the human heart,
> The flower of lovely youth that art;
> Yea, and that standest in thy youth
> An image of eternal Truth,
> With thy exuberant flesh so fair,
> That only Pheidias might compare.

The seventh line is strikingly effective. The word *exuberant* introduces an extra syllable into the line (it is a very light syllable, but it is not meant to be ignored or slurred) and thereby creates a moment of unexpected and delightful freedom. Here is an instance of a tiny variation creating an effect of great beauty. The extra syllable breaks the iambic meter, and because it is such a slight syllable, we race over it, and the speed gained heightens the effect of freedom still more. This metrical freedom matches the sense of the word *exuberant* and makes it evocative. The word refers, of course, to the god's joy and pride in flesh, but thanks to the buoyant effect that it creates in the meter, it also suggests the fact of Eros's *wings* (Eros is the ancestor of our modern Cupid). We get out of this modest metrical freedom, not only an aesthetic quality in the medium that corresponds to the idea being expressed, and makes that idea vivid, but also the suggestion of a visual image—the god's wings. The meter causes the abstract word *exuberant* to become wonderfully sensuous.

Students sometimes wonder whether a poet intends such subtleties or is even aware of them. Bridges was a careful and knowledgeable prosodist, and so we can be almost certain that in this case what we find is no lucky accident. But the question isn't really relevant to our experience of the poem. The poem is before us, and we can't deny our own responses: the effect of freedom and the suggestion of wings are there.

The eighth line of this passage has exactly the same metrical structure as the seventh, but in this case one can feel no particular correspondence between the idea and the meter; the deviation exists simply as desirable flexibility in the meter.

Many poets have been attracted to meter because it allows them, among other advantages, this kind of sensitive control of their medium, the words. It is obvious that the kinds of effects we have been examining here can't be rendered in free verse:

> From the living and the dead I think you have
> peopled your impassive surfaces, and the spirits
> thereof would be evident and amicable with me.

Where variation is the rule, no emphasis can be gained through the principle of variation from a normal pattern. But of course free verse has its own techniques.

VII. SECURING ATTENTION

In one sense, prosody is best understood as a technique for securing maximum attention. Not a few aestheticians consider the eliciting of a "wrapt attention" (to use the phrase of Eliseo Vivas) as one of the defining and most important characteristics of all aesthetic experience. Such attention is its own delight; we are seized by beauty and power, and part of our pleasure is in the being seized.

Meter, like the patterns of lining and of rhyme, and, on the semantic level, like themes and images, continually raises and continually satisfies *expectation*. The mind delights in anticipating a pattern. In poetry whose semantic and rhetorical virtues are what they should be, it helps draw the reader or listener in; it helps secure attention for what is there to be worthy of attention.

VIII. HEURISTIC FUNCTION

Meter may prove of direct and immediate value to a poet—and to his readers too—in another way. Juxtaposing words so that their stresses form a fairly regular pattern forces him to work with words as he ordinarily, in speaking, thinking, writing letters, writing prose, does not. This demand may lead him to discoveries he would not otherwise have made.

In writing a poem, a poet is constantly searching for words: ones that will express the poem's feeling and idea vividly, forcefully. The words he considers, then, must fit the *sense*. But if he is writing verse, the poet must find a word that also fits the meter; even the free verse poet, if he has a sensitive ear, will usually reject a word that fits the sense but mars the rhythm he wants. And searching for such a word may result in the discovery of one that makes richer or otherwise more interesting the meaning that the poet originally had in mind. The descent of such a word may even cause him to give a different, and possibly superior, turn to all that has come before. It even happens that a poet sometimes reaches a point, in working his way toward a finished poem, where his energy and imagination seem exhausted, where he remains frustrated, unable to get further. At such a point, the mere search for a word or words that continue the meter may renew his vitality and sense of direction. Unfortunately this is an event one is powerless to illustrate, but the authors give testimony to the fact of such occurrences, however rare, both in their own work and in that of other writers who have talked about their experience.

We may think of this as the HEURISTIC value of meter. In searching for words and phrases that will fit the formal requirement of the meter, a poet may—and no doubt frequently does—hit upon a happy word that might not otherwise have occurred to him. In a few glorious instances, that one word or phrase may even suggest new and usable ideas and images. It is a case of the meter actually bringing about meaning.

Formal restrictions can be valuable in other ways; those imposed by prosody, by an organization in terms of distinct parts or divisions suggested by the nature of the theme or story itself, or by conventions and limitations such as are encountered in the theatre—in every case, the freedom curtailed may mean an excellence gained. Shakespeare comes to mind at once. On his stage, and in his sonnets, he was firmly bound by all sorts of formal and thematic considerations. But in his erotic narrative *Venus and Adonis* he was free to write until his own imagination cloyed him, choosing a six-line stanza for the story and at the same time eschewing any part-divisions. He was free, too free, letting his fancy dally with the lascivious Venus fully as elaborately as the goddess dallies with the reluctant Adonis. The poem keeps its virtue; it is delightful and charming; but it suffers— as the plays themselves sometimes do, despite the economizing influence of convention and of theatrical crudity—from excess. The portrait is too full here, the speech too long there.

IX.   ORDER

Earlier we suggested that meter is probably as much an expression of order or rationality as of emotion.

In a successful poem, the poet presents some *understanding* of the experience he is dealing with: he brings a certain order or logic into play, adjusting his own attitude and feeling to suit his understanding of the subject or experience he is writing about. A good poem is thus unified, harmonious; and the regularity of meter can fit beautifully into such a scheme.

Lascelles Abercrombie has pointed out that the orderliness of meter is appropriate to tragic plays because in high tragedy the characters themselves—the protagonists and other dignified characters, at least—are somewhat simplified and patterned. The structure of the play is itself, of course, more ordered than real life, since the dramatist cuts out what is not essential in some way to his vision or theme. Highly ordered speech does not seem so "unnatural" in a highly ordered situation. The situation accommodates the meter, and the meter accommodates the situation.

X.   MNEMONIC VALUE

Verse sticks in the mind better than prose or free verse. The stress pattern helps us remember the word pattern. This mnemonic value of meter is so obvious and universally recognized as to require no discussion. It is probably true, too, that any rhythm tends to become more memorable as it becomes more regular. In ancient times and in the Middle Ages, when books (in any sense of the term) were rare, there was of necessity a greater reliance upon memory, and consequently whatever enhanced the mnemonic quality of a poem was welcome. In this regard, the value of meter, of whatever sort, is not to be underestimated. A minstrel would seldom have the money for a book, and even a marquis might find lean pickings at any price. The invention of printing gave a tremendous impetus to the development of prose—which had hitherto always lagged behind poetry, like the weak and uncertain son of a powerful father.

Meter seems to have a good many uses. We have tried to indicate some of the more obvious and important of them, and also a few that are often neglected, perhaps for no good reason. We have not, however, tried to be exhaustive, and we have not treated the functions of meter according to any order of importance. Obviously any given metrical function may be apparent and extremely important in one poem, and hardly worth noticing in another.

9
Tempo

The speed or tempo of lines varies greatly. Here is a swift line:

Or dip their pinions in the painted bow,

and here is an enormously slow line in the same meter:

With what deep murmurs through time's silent stealth.

In Chapter 3 we noted briefly certain characteristics of the syllable that tend to make a line quick or slow. We might now make a fuller synopsis of the various ways of slowing a line down or speeding it up. They apply, of course, to phrases and sentences of prose, as well as to lines of verse.

The line will be slower if it contains

1.   *An image or idea of slowness or rest.* The appropriate effect is produced even if—as in the following line—few of the syllables are intrinsically long, and there is no other reason why the line should move slowly:

Resting weary limbs at last on beds of asphodel.

2.   *Difficulty of articulation.* A line of verse that from syllable to syllable constantly forces the vocal organs to reshape themselves —as from alternation between back and front, and open and closed vowels, and between dissimilar consonant sounds—will tend to be slow paced. There is no improving on Pope's brilliant example:

When Ajax strives some rock's vast weight to throw.

3.   *Diaeresis.* When the beginnings and endings of the feet correspond to the beginnings and endings of words:

In doubt | to deem | himself | a god, | or beast.

4.   *Successive stresses.*

As a dáre-gále skylárk scánted in a dúll cáge.

5.   *Predominance of long syllables.*

Avenge, O Lord, thy slaughtered saints, whose bones.

6.   *Caesuras.*

Cover her face: mine eyes dazzle: she died young.

7.   *Monosyllabism.* Other things being equal, a line in which words of one syllable predominate will be slower than a line containing a number of polysyllables:

Thrice she looked back, and thrice the foe drew near.

8.   *Hiatus.* Hiatus, literally "a break," comes about when the end of one syllable and the beginning of the next have the same or a quite similar sound. Traditionally, the term has been employed to designate only the situation in which identical vowels abutt; however, the etymology of the word suits it as well for the case of abutting consonants:

No open door: we eased back the way you did.

With what deep murmurs through time's silent stealth.

To get the enunciation clear, it is necessary to pause slightly between such syllables.

The line will move faster if it shows none of the above characteristics and if it does show such characteristics as alliteration, internal rhyme, trisyllabic feet (dactyls and anapests), and a predominance of words of more than one syllable.

10
Rhyme

RHYME is agreement in sound between words or syllables. The agreement may range from exact correspondence (*rhyme–rhyme*) to correspondence at one or more points (*rhyme–time; rhyme–room; rhyme–sky; rhyme–risk; deciding–deriding; mention–convention*). This is the widest sense of the word, and a very useful sense. Today, however, a narrower one is customary: when we speak of rhyme, we usually have in mind only two types of agreement: different initial sounds and identical following sounds (*rhyme–time*), or polysyllables which correspond at every point except one (*deciding–deriding; massively–passively*).

English poetry is overwhelmingly a poetry of rhyme. Old English poetry used rhyme in the form we call ALLITERATION: agreement in consonant sounds at the beginning of words:

> *b*runfagne *h*elm, *h*ringde *b*yrnan.

> (shining helmet, ring byrny.)

The alliterative line was the basis of much Middle English poetry as well:

> Justed ful jolilé thise gentyle knightes.

From Chaucer onward, however, END RHYME became the dominant type and is the only kind used extensively today. Even some free verse makes use of rhyme; we noticed it—both full rhyme and alliteration—in the opening lines of Whitman's "When Lilacs Last in the Dooryard Bloom'd," and more recently certain free verse poets (Louis Zukofsky and Robert Creeley, for example) have sometimes worked it rather extensively into their poems. Like meter, rhyme has persisted because it can be useful and, sometimes, even indispensable. But before we consider its uses we need to say something more about the various *kinds* of rhyme. It is convenient to distinguish four types: (1) full rhyme (or simply rhyme), (2) slant rhyme (sometimes called half rhyme or off rhyme), (3) alliteration, and (4) assonance.

One preliminary remark is necessary: when we speak of rhyme as agreement or partial agreement in sound, we imply that this agreement is being used as a conscious device, that it is intended to be conspicuous. We find *some* rhyme—in the wide sense of the term—in almost any line of poetry, since getting the right sense will frequently result in a degree of alliteration or assonance. In many lines, then, we discover fortuitous agreement among sounds. Here, for example, is a couplet from the fourth Canto of Pope's "Rape of the Lock":

> Unnumbered throngs on every side are seen,
> Of bodies changed to various forms by Spleen.

There are a good many s- and z-sounds in these lines, but their occurrence is of no particular significance. They are unobtrusive; we scarcely notice the preponderance unless we happen to analyze the lines. On the other hand, here are two lines by Tennyson which contain about the same number of s- and z-sounds, distributed in about the same way:

> There is sweet music here that softer falls
> Than petals from blown roses on the grass.

Why do we notice Tennyson's sibilance but not Pope's? The answer seems to be that we are likely to feel such alliteration or assonance as an aesthetic effect only when the sense of the line invites it. In poetry, sound and sense are intimately connected. Sound can strengthen or emphasize meaning and feeling; meaning and feeling can make the sounds more evocative. The second process is not often enough brought to our attention. We are always told that poets use alliteration to bind important words together to secure the most intense unity of meaning or feeling ("the flashing foam"), or to create onomatopoeia (as in the Tennyson lines above). The statement is perfectly true, but it is also important to see that the alliterated words must already exist in some sort of logical relationship before alliteration will bind them, or they must already suggest a certain idea or quality of feeling before we feel the sound agreements helping to suggest that idea or feeling.

The intentional use of rhyme—in any of its forms—also implies that the rhyming words or syllables are relatively close to one another. If the first and seventeenth lines of a poem alliterate *s*, we are not likely to notice the connection. Milton's unrhymed *Paradise Lost* actually contains a good many lines whose final words rhyme, but usually the rhymes are so far apart as to produce no aesthetic effect. We are not likely to feel end rhyme at intervals of more than four or five lines.

I.   FULL RHYME

This is normal, standard, ordinary rhyme: *sing–ring*. Initially unlike sounds are followed by like sounds, or, in the case of certain polysyllables, there is agreement at all points except one: *invention–mention*. And what if the same words, or what if homonyms, are brought together: *love–love, fate–fete?* One occasionally sees a repeat or a homonym rhyme, but they are rare. They are almost always either monotonous or comic, and both effects limit their use. Nevertheless there is no reason not to count them as full rhyme.

Rhymes are MASCULINE or FEMININE. All monosyllable rhymes are masculine: *turn–learn, stone–bone*. Rhyming words of two or more syllables are masculine if the final syllables are the stressed ones: *respect–collect*. Such rhyme is called masculine because it gives an effect of strength not present in rhymes in which the stressed and rhyming syllables are followed by unstressed syllables.

A rhyme such as *land–contraband* is masculine even though

con- rather than *-band* receives the primary stress. The secondary stress of *-band* is strong enough to give the masculine force. Rhyme involving final syllables of secondary stress, then, usually seems masculine.

Feminine rhymes are rhyming words of two or more syllables in which the stressed and rhymed syllables are not the final ones: *spiteful–rightful, merrily–warily, indestructible–ineluctable.* "Feminine" because the absence of stress and the drop in pitch toward the end of the word give a light or weak effect.

Some writers distinguish a third type: WEAK RHYME, a kind of rhyme in which the rhyming syllables are unstressed or very lightly stressed: *voluminous–incredulous, father–color.* Weak rhyme is rare and is almost nonexistent in English poetry before the twentieth century.

Rhyme may occur at the ends of lines (TERMINAL RHYME), at the beginnings (INITIAL RHYME), or within the line (INTERNAL RHYME). Terminal or end rhyme is by far the most common, and initial rhyme is extremely rare.

> Had we but world enough, and *time,*
> This coyness, lady, were no *crime.*

> ⁓

> Little here has changed, least of all, the *gulls*
> mewing over flotsam, scouting harbor,
> sleep of *hulls* and guanoed cobblestone.

> ⁓

> *Wind* the whirlpool
> *Blind* and certain;
> *Dark* as the dark there,
> *Stark,* you shall disturb.

Until very recent times internal rhyme almost always followed a certain pattern: a word near or at the middle of the line rhymed with the last word of the line:

> Ah, distinctly I remember it was in the bleak December.

Such rhyme is only technically internal, since it really has the effect of breaking the line into two lines. In many such cases, as in this line from Poe's "The Raven," it is difficult to see any point in joining the two lines as if they were one. Here, however, is an instance of internal rhyme that does not break the line:

> Upon the supreme theme of Art and Song.

II.   SLANT RHYME

Synonyms are *near rhyme, oblique rhyme, half rhyme, off rhyme*. Slant rhymes are approximate rhymes, and the possible varieties are very numerous. Here are only a few possibilities of slant rhyme with the word "blink"

> (*i*)   *blink–blank*
> (*ii*)   *blink–blip*
> (*iii*) *blink–thank*
> (*iv*)   *blink–bleak*
> (*v*)   *blink–brisk*

The vowel sound only may be changed (*i, iii*) or one of the consonant sounds (*ii*) or more than one consonant sound (*v*) or the vowel and one or more—but not all—of the consonant sounds (*iv*). To coin separate terms for each type of slant rhyme is a work of supererogation.

This type of rhyming was relatively rare in English poetry until the twentieth century. It is found with some frequency, however, in the poetry of William Blake and Emily Dickinson. It abounds in the verse of Wilfrid Owen, W. B. Yeats, and W. H. Auden.

The exact effect of slant rhyme is difficult to describe, and of course different kinds have somewhat different effects. It is not nearly as pleasing to the ear, and sometimes it is undeniably dissonant. Its harshness or dissonance is at once its strength and its limitation. It frustrates the ear by coming close to the melodic quality of rhyme without resolving into it. Hence it is suitable for poems in which any form of euphony would be disastrous. Notice how it helps create a tone of despair and anxiety in the following lines from Wilfrid Owen's war poem "Arms and the Boy":

> Let the boy try along this bayonet-blade
> How cold steel is, and keen with hunger of blood;
> Blue with all malice, like a madman's flash;
> And thinly drawn with famishing for flesh.

The ugly connotations of the rhyming words, along with the brutal tone of the whole quatrain, undoubtedly make the rhyme seem even more dissonant than it is. At the same time, the rhymes themselves are like unresolved or dissonant chords.

Yeats frequently employed slant rhyme simply because ours is not a rhyme-rich language. At other times he used it to suggest and complement harshness of image or feeling, as in these lines:

> Till all her bowels are in heat,
> Proof that there's a purpose set.

In the lines below the rhyme suits the image of brutal sexual fulfillment:

> Belly, shoulder, bum,
> Flash fishlike; nymphs and satyrs
> Copulate in the foam.

Because of the dissonant quality of this kind of rhyme, and because ours is a tradition of full rather than of slant rhyme, consistent slant rhyme tends to seem highly artificial: it throws great emphasis upon the rhyming words, and becomes a banal and pretentious device when there is no reason for such emphasis and when nothing in the spirit of the poem demands an avoidance of melody. Here, however, is a stanza from Yeats's poem "The Municipal Gallery Revisited" in which the slant rhymes are so faint that they are no more obtrusive than ordinary rhymes:

> Heart-smitten with emotion I sink down,
> My heart recovering with covered eyes;
> Wherever I had looked I had looked upon
> My permanent or impermanent images:
> Augusta Gregory's son; her sister's son,
> Hugh Lane, 'onlie begetter' of all these;
> Hazel Lavery living and dying, that tale
> As though some ballad-singer had sung it all.

This is much like blank verse; the diction, the syntax, and the quality of feeling are so natural that the rhyming goes on almost unnoticed.

Unlike ordinary rhyme, which is frequently internal and occasionally initial, slant rhyme is almost never (perhaps never, the writers know of no instances) used except as end rhyme. At the end of a line, where we expect to find full rhyme, slant rhyme is ordinarily extremely conspicuous, but anywhere else it is likely to be too faint a correspondence to attract any particular attention.

III.   ALLITERATION

Alliteration usually takes the form of agreement in consonant sounds at the beginnings of proximate words:

> As a *d*are-gale *sk*ylark *sc*anted in a *d*ull cage.

However, there is no reason why we should not regard as alliteration the sibilance of Tennyson's lines:

> There is sweet music here that softer falls
> Than petals from blown roses on the grass.

Not all of the *s* and *z* sounds come at the beginnings of words, but they certainly repeat so often as to be felt; they create a distinctive, dominating color. But the effect of such sound-repetition as we find here—occurring as it does among both stressed and unstressed syllables, and within words as well as at word beginnings—is usually different from the effect rendered by alliteration in the narrower sense. Tennyson's sibilance here produces onomatopoeia (in this case, of a rather generalized sort: a suggestion of mild atmospheres and lush, serene landscapes); Hopkins' alliteration "proper" does not. The kind of sound-repetition we get in the Tennyson lines tends not so much to throw individual *words* (and consequently images or ideas) into strong relief, as to diffuse a particular *tone* throughout the whole sequence of words. Notice, in this regard, how semantically active the alliteration is in the line by Hopkins. It makes the antithesis in idea the more striking: the *skylark* (free in its proper element) is *scanted* (confined in a cage); the bird that will *d*are *g*ales is to be clamped in a *d*ull *c*age (notice the vowel agreement between *gales* and *cage*). Alliteration was, incidentally, a favorite device of Hopkins, and he used it to better advantage than most other modern English poets. Swinburne, his contemporary, was notoriously fond of it too, but quite often his poems seem to exist *for the sake* of the alliteration.

In such a line as this, for example, from his poem "In a Rosary,"

> Roses like a rainbow wrought of roses rise,

the alliteration is so cloying that we could well wish the poet had never heard of the device.

Alliteration, then, tends to create a kind of discourse which focuses our attention minutely on the linguistic details of a sequence of words: it makes us feel the words, rather than race across them to get to the idea, as is our habit with prose (notice that we even take pains to avoid alliteration in prose, where it seems appropriate only for a humorous or an eccentric effect). This property of alliteration is advantageous to the poet, who is, after all, trying to create a kind of discourse in which individual words and rhythms are more vividly felt than is the case with prose. In Coleridge's words, it is essential that a poem possess "the property of exciting a more continuous and equal attention than the language of prose aims at" (*Biographia Literaria*, Chapter XIV). A further comment, from the same source and chapter, is too relevant and memorable to pass over:

> The reader should be carried forward, not merely or chiefly by the mechanical impulse of curiosity, or by a restless desire to arrive at the final solution; but by the pleasureable activity of the mind excited by the attractions of the journey itself . . . at every step he pauses and half recedes, and from the retrogressive movement collects the force which again carries him onward.

Alliteration finds its true home in poetry. It elicits unusual attention because it is something out of the ordinary, and perhaps because there is an innate psychological tendency, at least among sensitive readers, to notice repetitions of any sort. The mere effect of focusing attention is an important consideration: anything to hold a listener's attention. In the case of a long poem set in the oral tradition—in *Beowulf*, for example—the alliteration (made the more prominent by stress) must have played no small part in the total aesthetic effect on the audience. Its conspicuousness elicited attention; it gave pleasure both because it was a familiar technique (Hrothgar would have been shocked if he had been told that someday a poetry without alliteration would arise) and because it created order and pattern—qualities which human beings delight in at least as much as they delight in spontaneity and freedom. Finally, the alliteration bound words together which logically went together, thus making for both an emphatic quality and ease of apprehension.

Alliteration is also highly mnemonic: it is easier to remember

The *l*ong *l*ight shakes across the *l*akes

than

The strong light shakes across the ponds.

Who can forget the tongue-twisters?

She sells seashells by the seashore.

The opening line of *Piers Plowman* gives us an example of alliteration that both binds words together logically—thereby helping to create a quite active context—and results in onomatopoeic quality:

In a somer season when softe was the sonne . . .

The softness of the alliterating *s*s is highly appropriate to the sense.

As in the case of meter, from the poet's point of view alliteration may sometimes prove *heuristic*. If a poet has decided to work in an alliterative form, then the need to find words with certain sound patterns may stimulate the mind and may lead to felicities of content that would not otherwise have occurred to him. Even to a verbally gifted and imaginative mind like the poet's, a fresh and brilliant epithet like "dare-gale" is much less likely to occur than a more conventional phrase like "dull cage." The latter is ready to hand; but if the poet has decided to draw heavily on alliteration, searching for something to go with it may well lead to a gale-daring skylark. Alliteration can also help a poet get on with his work in another way: an alliterative pattern, like any other, provides the poet with a guideline—and knowing precisely what is expected of one is a good preparation for performing it.

Alliteration is not without its disadvantages. Like ordinary rhyme, it is easy to make and is therefore dangerous. Its conspicuousness is its potential weakness as well as its strength. Of the language of a great many poems, it may be said that conspicuousness is its only virtue. The making of showy, jingling, trivial verse has no end. In the twentieth century, most English poetry has shied well away from alliteration, even when it has held onto rhyme. This exorcising is partly a reaction against the alliterating nineteenth century, and partly a more positive desire to head poetry in the direction of prose and of informality.

IV.   ASSONANCE

Assonance is to vowels what alliteration is to consonants: agreement or near agreement of nearby vowel sounds, especially at the beginnings of words or at stressed syllables within words. We have already seen assonance in the long *a*s of Hopkins' *gale* and *cage*. Here are some additional examples:

(*i*)   *I*nd*i*st*i*nct *i*n h*i*s *i*mperfect sight.

(*ii*)   The bl*u*e Mediterr*a*nean, where he l*a*y,
Lulled by the coil of his crystalline streams,
Beside a pumice *i*sle in B*a*iae's b*a*y.

Assonance can create beautiful melodic effects, as in (*ii*) above. Notice there, also, the alliteration and the liquidity and sibilance—a number of patterns going together to create an extraordinary but not cloying euphony.

When assonance is used as the basis of end rhyme, it is usually called T E R M I N A L   A S S O N A N C E:

Over blue st*o*ne
Blue water fl*ow*s,
And clouds in the bl*ue*
Silence of the deep t*u*ne.

The lines of Dylan Thomas's "Poem in October," quoted in part in Chapter 6, mate in an extremely intricate pattern of terminal assonance; the effect is richly lyrical and not at all strained.

11

The Uses of Rhyme

I. RHYME AND ATTENTION

When things work out as they should, a work of art—be it a poem, a play, a picture, a sonata—elicits our *complete attention*. In fact, this condition of "wrapt attention," as Eliseo Vivas has termed it, is one of the essential characteristics of all aesthetic experience. We are *held*. Rhyme, at the same time that it is performing various other functions, helps rivet our attention. A pattern of parallels in sound color is set up, and as we move through the poem, whether in reading or in listening, our expectation is continually being raised and then satisfied. Ideally, rhyme helps pull us through and pull us in deeper, as we anticipate the scheme. This principle holds true even in the case of a highly irregular arrangement of the rhyme words: we still feel ahead, expecting the sound colors to find their mates *somewhere*. Meter, refrains, and all other parallel or repeated elements work to the same advantage.

If the rhyme words are also completely effective—completely flawless in terms of *meaning*, logically and imaginatively right—then they are also integral parts of the poem's vitality, and not simply a

96

mechanical convenience; they are not then ornaments, but part of the very tissue.

II.   MUSICAL QUALITY

Rhyme creates an effect which is pleasing and satisfying and which, by analogy, is traditionally referred to as musical or melodic quality.

Euphonious rhymes (e.g., *full–wool*) are undoubtedly felt as more melodic than others, but since a certain pleasure comes about as a result of the mere fact of *agreement*, even words of harsh quality (*scratch–batch*) seem to lose some of their harshness in the pleasure that comes about when they are rhymed.

Rhyme is thus a source of acoustic pleasure, and this pleasure will exist in any rhyming poem, independently of anything else in it. This pleasure, the tone or emotional coloring created by rhyme, may be described if not very accurately defined by words such as charm, sweetness, and harmony. But, to repeat, this musicality derives from the sheer *fact* of rhyme, whether or not the words themselves are mellifluous. The effect is not rendered by slant rhyme.

Consequently, rhyme seems particularly suitable in poems that in some way celebrate spiritual or sensuous beauty or love, or that express repose or the satisfaction of self-control or even the satisfaction that can come from discovering something about the world or about one's self. "Realist" modern poets—William Carlos Williams and Carl Sandburg, for example—instinctively avoid rhyme.

In each of the following four passages, the music of the rhyme in some way complements the ideas and feelings expressed:

(*i*)   Come unto these yellow sands,
  And then take hands.
 Curtsied when you have and kissed,
  The wild waves whist,
 Foot it featly here and there;
 And, sweet sprites, the burthen bear.

(*ii*)   And still she slept an azure-lidded sleep.
 In blanched linen, smooth and lavendered,

> While he from forth the closet brought a heap
> Of candied apple, quince, and plum, and gourd;
> With jellies soother than the creamy curd,
> And lucent syrops, tinct with cinnamon;
> Manna and dates, in argosy transferred
> From Fez; and spiced dainties, every one,
> From silken Samarcand to cedared Lebanon.

(*iii*)   It is a beauteous evening, calm and free;
      The holy time is quiet as a nun
      Breathless with adoration; the broad sun
      Is sinking down in its tranquility;
      The gentleness of heaven broods o'er the sea.

(*iv*)   Beauty is but a flower
      Which wrinkles will devour:
      Brightness falls from the air,
      Queens have died young and fair,
      Dust hath closed Helen's eye.
      I am sick, I must die.
        Lord, have mercy upon us!

It is easy to see that whatever sheerly musical pleasure we find in rhyme can only make Ariel's song (*i*) more songlike. In the Keats passage (*ii*), rhyme music is completely appropriate to the sense-delighting images so lovingly dwelt upon. And rhyme is no less complementary to the experience of wonder and serenity presented in the Wordsworth lines (*iii*). But what is to prevent the pleasurableness of rhyme from conflicting with such distinctly painful and ascetic feeling as is expressed in (*iv*), a stanza from Thomas Nashe's "Litany"? We noticed earlier, too, the rhyming in the first few lines of Whitman's elegy "When Lilacs Last in the Dooryard Bloom'd," and in Milton's most intensely emotional sonnet "On the Late Massacre in Piedmont". Yet we would not change a syllable in any of these poems.

The reason that rhyme can be as appropriate to darker as to brighter expression is, first, that musicality is after all only one effect of rhyme, and that rhyme itself is only one element in the poem.

Any one or any number of the several other functions of rhyme, which coexist with its melodic quality, may be so important that any musical effect will be all but canceled out. And in a successful poem the impact of image and idea will be more impressive than the impact of the rhyme itself. Finally we have to remember the principle that the *meaning* of a line will influence our response to its sound pattern: some of our delight in the blithe reveling of Ariel's song seems to carry over to the rhymes, coloring them with more pleasure than we would perceive if we found the same rhymes in a more somber context. In Nashe's stanza the rhyme is more than justified by its various functions. For example, it helps make each thought, even each line, more emphatic and more memorable by setting it apart; it strengthens an antithesis (*flower* and *devour*); and it makes the word *air* more conspicuous and thereby more evocative, the word connoting the idea of the fall of lofty, aspiring beauty; of the failing of sight at the moment of death; of the necessity of air and of its foulness and contagion in plague time.

In the stanzas below, the poet seems to have decided that rhyme music is the most important element in verse:

Searching for strawberries ready to eat,
Finding them crimson and large and sweet,
What do you think I found at my feet—
    Deep in the green hill-side?

Four brown sparrows, the cunning things,
Feathered on back and breast and wings,
Proud with the dignity plumage brings,
    Opening their four mouths wide.

But readers have decided otherwise. There is no intensity of meaning or feeling to justify the obtrusiveness of the triplet rhyme, and the rhyming words themselves seem to have been chosen for their rhyme value at the expense of meaning and economy and rhetorical stress. The whole phrase *the cunning things* is mere redundancy and padding, and the word *brings* receives illogical rhetorical prominence and is redundant also. "Proud with the dignity of plumage" would be better.

To sum up, rhyme creates a musical effect that, in a good

poem, is always pleasurable, and that is therefore especially suited to poems that express some pleasure of human experience. But pleasure is inherent even in the act of understanding, and since most poems present the poet's understanding of his experience, rhyme seldom seems inappropriate.

III.   BINDING OR ARCHITECTURAL QUALITY

Rhyme can help to unify words and groups of lines that belong together. When the idea or tone or basic image or metaphor changes, a change in rhyme sounds may signal it. Notice the rhyme structure of this Shakespeare sonnet;

> That time of year thou mayst in me behold
> When yellow leaves, or none, or few, do hang
> Upon those boughs which shake against the cold,
> Bare ruin'd choirs where late the sweet birds sang.
> In me thou see'st the twilight of such day
> As after sunset fadeth in the West,
> Which by-and-by black night doth take away,
> Death's second self, that seals up all in rest.
> In me thou see'st the glowing of such fire
> That on the ashes of his youth doth lie,
> As the deathbed whereon it must expire,
> Consum'd with that which it was nourish'd by.
>   This thou perceiv'st, which makes thy love more strong,
>   To love that well which thou must leave ere long.

The organization of this sonnet is simple and effective: three quatrains and a concluding couplet. Each quatrain elaborates a metaphor of decay: a winter-stripped tree; sunset; a dying fire. The couplet then relates the metaphors to a specific human situation and brings the poem to its point. The rhyme-sound patterns change with the changes in metaphor, and each of the four sections, being thus set off, becomes more distinct, more emphatic. It is likely too that the harking-back effect of the rhymes helps us remember the succeeding images and ideas more vividly and thus to experience the poem more intensely.

IV. RHYME FOR EMPHASIS

Rhyme makes a word conspicuous, and since rhyme already normally occurs at a position of rhetorical prominence—the end of a line—rhyming words need to be important words in the meaning of the line. In the poem below, Shelley takes full advantage of the emphasis made possible by rhyme:

> Music, when soft voices die,
> Vibrates in the memory—
> Odours, when sweet violets sicken,
> Live within the sense they quicken.
>
> Rose leaves, when the rose is dead,
> Are heap'd for the beloved's bed;
> And so thy thoughts, when thou art gone,
> Love itself shall slumber on.

Each pair of rhymes is related logically as well as acoustically, and the resulting strength is impressive. The logical relationship here is, for the most part, that of antithesis. Singing voices *die* but live on in the *memory*, violets wither or *sicken*, but their odor has made life *quicken* in the persons near them.

In Robert Bridges' poem "Nightingales" the singing birds become symbols of artists—poets, musicians, painters—who are always painfully aware of the gap between their expression (the song) and the yet more beautiful vision and deeper and richer complex of feeling that lie within, unexpressed:

> Our song is the voice of desire, that haunts our dreams,
>   A throe of the heart,
> Whose pining visions dim, forbidden hopes profound,
>   No dying cadence nor long sigh can sound
>   For all our art.

Here too the rhymes are logically, as well as acoustically, prominent. To *sound* means to utter; it also means, as in navigation, to probe to the floor or bottom. We would lose this latter meaning if the word did not mate with *profound*, which also means *deep*. And from any point of view, both words are key words. *Heart* and *art* pair with the same effectiveness: rhyme helps strengthen the idea of the inevitable disparity between desire and attainment, vision and utterance.

V.   HEURISTIC QUALITY

We have already said something about the heuristic value of meter. Rhyme too can be heuristic; it can help directly in the birth and growth of a poem.

The poet's decision to follow a set rhyme scheme or even to rhyme in some irregular fashion, limits his choice of words. Such a limitation may, of course, be maddening and may result in complete frustration or in shoddy verse.

On the other hand, aside from the requirements of meaning, this limitation frees the mind from the near-infinity of vocabulary and allows the poem to proceed. Ideally a rhyme sets the imagination (and free association) to work until the poet comes up with an image or turn of thought that fits the sense as well as the sound. A rhyme may even bring an image or idea that will suggest a new line of development. At its best, rhyme leads the poet into discoveries.

In Yeats's poem "Sailing to Byzantium" there is an unmistakable instance of the heuristic value of rhyme. The most impressive single effect in this poem is the repetition, at the end of the final stanza, of a rhyme that ended the poem's second stanza. In the exact center of the poem are the lines:

> And therefore I have sailed the seas and come
> To the holy city of Byzantium.

And at the very end,

> . . . upon a golden bough to sing
> To lords and ladies of Byzantium
> Of what is past, or passing, or to come.

This resonant rhyme sends a vibration back through the whole poem, enhancing its vitality, and at the same time concluding it on a stronger note than it would have had otherwise. Obviously one couplet suggested the other.

Much of the vitality of Robert Frost's poem "Departmental," about the efficiency of ants, depends on the wit and surprise created in the rhyming words:

> Then word goes forth in Formic:
> Death's come to Jerry McCormic,
> Our selfless forager Jerry.
> Will the special Janizary
> Whose office it is to bury
> The dead of the commissary
> Go bring him home to his people.

The brilliance here is largely a result of a deliberate strain or tension between ideas emphatically juxtaposed by rhyme. The unexpected but splendid image of the Janizary, and the delightful conjunction of "Formic" and "McCormic" owe their existence to Frost's decision to rhyme.

The heuristic importance of rhyme was explored in some detail by Hegel but more quotably by Henry Lanz (*The Physical Basis of Rhyme*), who put it this way:

> it often happens that rime precedes and produces the idea. . . . Even words which are but distantly related may be successfully put together into a phrase provided a sufficient number of mediating words are given to connect them. Occasionally such artificial unions may result in unexpected sayings and even in great discoveries . . . there are, so to speak, many underground passages leading from one word to another. The poet often roams in darkness until an ingenious rime helps him out into the light.

VI.   FORMALITY OF RHYME

Like meter, rhyme is a highly formal device. It is a signal that language is going to be used in an unusual, often a serious and memorable, way. In Alfred Hayes' poem "The Slaughter-House" irregularly employed rhyme is just sufficient to raise the tone of a language that is otherwise very close to prose. It lends dignity and memorableness to the expression—

> Under the big 500-watted lamps, in the huge sawdusted government
>   inspected slaughter-house,
> head down from hooks and clamps, run on trolleys over troughs,
> the animals die.
> Whatever terror their dull intelligences feel
>   or what agony distorts their most protruding eyes
> the incommunicable narrow skulls conceal.
>   Across the sawdusted floor,
> ignorant as children, they see the butcher's slow
>   methodical approach
> in the bloodied apron, leather cap above, thick square shoes below,
> struggling to comprehend this unique vision upside down,
> and then approximate a human scream
>   as from the throat slit like a letter
> the blood empties, and the windpipe, like a blown valve, spurts steam.

Because it is out of the ordinary, rhyme attracts our attention
and prepares us for a completely organized and unusually expressive
language. The functions of rhyme in attracting our attention and
holding it from one musical expectation to another, and of creating
a sense of order and a heightened tone appropriate to the highly
selective and highly organized experience poems usually present, are
of no small importance.

VII. AESTHETIC DISTANCE

Rhyme can help a poet get the aesthetic distance he needs in
order to write at all of a subject in which he is intimately involved,
and which threatens to overwhelm him with paralyzing emotion as he
contemplates it and tries to write of it in the most straightforward
way. The necessity of constructing rhyme may in some cases force
the poet to move the original experience just far enough to the rear
of the immediate feelings involved that he will be able to write about
it or some sea-changed aspect of it, without sentimentality or the
enervating sense of futility that sometimes results from a realization
of the great disparity between the vividness and depth of an original
experience and the expression of it or any part of it in verse.

Rhyme, as Wordsworth suggested, creates aesthetic distance
for the reader too. Sorrow in verse gives us an experience of some-

thing we call beauty, not of the sorrow the poet might have felt at one time, and not the sorrow we would feel in actual life if we were to have the experience the poem deals with. If it were not for the aesthetic distance created by formal elements such as meter and rhyme, and by the general eloquence of expression, we would respond to every poem and play and story in much the same way we would respond to the corresponding situations in real experience. When we are engrossed in a suspenseful novel in which the hero, with whom we have identified ourselves, is about to fall victim to the villain, our pulse may quicken a bit, but we do not turn pale or run out of the room to cry for help. The situation and the language in Alfred Hayes' "The Slaughter-House" are so brutal and repugnant that some slight thread of conscious artifice—the rhyme—seems to be needed, or at least welcomed, to turn into poetry an experience which is unpleasant enough even when vicarious. It seems to be a fact that the more pleasant or dignified, noble or beautiful the subject or experience of a poem, the more easily we can do without such artifices as rhyme and meter (although, paradoxically, such subjects and experiences make the *music* of rhyme and meter most appropriate). Lovely imagery, passionate imagination, and warm or lofty sentiment are their own rewards: it is much more difficult to bring off a poem which presents unpleasant matter in unpleasant language. Only a perverse and amateurish artist, or only an immature one, supposes that sane people will, over a period of years and generations, so violate their human nature as to indulge in ugliness or pain for its own sake. Ugliness must be made attractive and endurable—as Rouault often made his prostitutes and degenerates endurable by the luminosity and delicious coolness of his color. The more a poem deals in guts and gutters, the more we appreciate the aesthetic distance of rhymes and iambs.

VII. MNEMONIC QUALITY

The power of rhyme to drive its way into the memory is too well known to dwell on. Rhyming verse is the most memorable of all possible linguistic constructions, and rhyme in any situation is a positive aid to memory. One of its more famous uses as a pedagogic device was the eighteenth-century *New England Primer:*

> *G* As runs the Glass,
>   Our life doth pass.

ॐ

Impart your portion to the poor,
   in money and in meat
And send the feeble fainting soul,
   of that which you do eat.

12
The Stanza

In prose a group of sentences related to a single idea—and so related closely to one another—is called a paragraph. Each paragraph develops an idea that is in some way related to the main idea of the composition. Paragraphing is logical and convenient: it signals the beginning of a new idea or a change in tone, it allows us to see more easily the relationships among the various ideas and consequently to gain a sense of direction, and it provides welcome visual relief from what would otherwise be a frighteningly solid block of print. A stanza is the verse equivalent of a paragraph. Like each paragraph in a story or essay, a stanza advances the composition; again like the paragraph, an individual stanza may represent a complete change in tone and idea or only a very slight one.

Like many other prosodic terms, the word stanza has been very loosely used. Some writers have restricted it to mean only regularly recurring groups of lines of the same number. Others have used it to refer to almost any group set off typographically from the poem as a whole. This latter usage has the virtue of inclusiveness and eliminates the need for separate terms. Of course a poem of a thousand lines broken into, say, three groups, the first of 200, the second of 500, and the third of 300 lines, may not properly be said to have stanzas, since we always find in such large groups more than a single idea developed. A suitable term would be the one we are already using—group; section and division are also useful terms.

Edmund Waller's "Go, Lovely Rose" contains four five-line stanzas:

> Go, lovely Rose—
> Tell her that wastes her time and me
>   That now she knows,
> When I resemble her to thee,
> How sweet and fair she seems to be.
>
>   Tell her that's young,
> And shuns to have her graces spied,
>   That hadst thou sprung
> In deserts where no men abide,
> Thou must have uncommended died.
>
>   Small is the worth
> Of beauty from the light retired:
>   Bid her come forth,
> Suffer herself to be desired,
> And not blush so to be admired.
>
>   Then die—that she
> The common fate of all things rare
>   May read in thee:
> How small a part of time they share
> That are so wondrous sweet and fair.

The first stanza introduces the love situation, using the rose as a symbol. But the exact nature of the situation and the exact symbolism of the rose and the message it will perhaps carry to the girl are not reasonably clear until the end of the second stanza, and are not, in fact, fully clear until the very end of the poem. The ideas elaborated in the second and third stanzas are much alike, but by no means identical. Furthermore, the stanzas are arranged in an order of climax; any rearrangement would be ruinous.

The stanzas of Waller's lyric are formal, regular, symmetrical. Many formal stanzas have evolved or been adopted in English verse, are known by various names, and range in size from two lines—called a couplet or distich—to many. In the next chapter we shall note some of the traditional stanza forms and their characteristics.

Each stanza in "Go, Lovely Rose" consists of lines that vary in length: the initial line is dimeter, the next is tetrameter, then dimeter again, then two more tetrameters. With few exceptions (notably the ballad stanza) stanzas in which there is a pattern of varying line lengths have not been given names. They are often called "song" forms, sometimes "free" forms. There are many such stanzas, more, in fact, than one could find plausible names for, and of course the number of possible combinations of rhyme-scheme and line-length patterns is astronomical. In general, stanzas in which the line lengths remain the same have been in more frequent use, and this familiarity is in many cases what accounts for their having been christened.

Despite their variations in length of line, the Waller stanzas are symmetrical—the variations follow a predictable pattern. Nearly all formal stanzas show such symmetry between stanza and stanza, and this is not pedantry or mere love of order for order's sake. Once the poet has set up a pattern, he is obliged to continue it. We begin to move in the pattern and we expect that scheme again and again. Should there be a deviation—suppose that Waller had made the third line of his third stanza a pentameter instead of the anticipated dimeter —the speed and whole nature of our movement would necessarily change at that point, and conscious of the change, we should ask ourselves why such a change had occurred. If we discover no reason, we feel that our expectations have been disappointed capriciously, and the poem is marred.

But, one hastens to add, there may well be a good reason. Since the stanza establishes a normal pattern in which variations will become conspicuous and hence emphatic, the poet can create special effects by altering that pattern. Here are the first three lines of Hopkins' sonnet "God's Grandeur":

> The world is charged with the grandeur of God;
> It will flame out, like shining from shook foil;
> It gathers to a greatness, like the ooze of oil.

The third line is a hexameter instead of the expected pentameter, and the increase in length suggests the meaning of the line: the line itself "gathers to a greatness" and being long suggests the slowness of the oozing oil.

An increase or decrease in line length, or a change in rhyme scheme, is a major variation, and relatively rare in poems that employ the stanza. It tends to unbalance a poem by making one stanza seem more striking than the others—to mar it by interrupting our pleasure in expectation and fulfillment. Successful poems are written in a particular stanza that is itself expressive of their thought and feeling, and consequently precludes the necessity of major variations.

13
Stanza Forms

I. THE COUPLET

The simplest of English stanzas is the couplet:

Phryne
Thy flattering picture, Phryne, is like thee,
Only in this, that you both painted be.

A poem may consist of a single couplet, like the Donne epigram above, or of a series of couplets. An unrhymed stanza of two lines—a rare form in English—is called an unrhymed couplet or a DISTICH.

Iambic tetrameter and pentameter couplets are by far the most common. Any group of lines that rhyme consecutively rather than alternately, however, are properly described as couplets. Thus Shelley's "Music When Soft Voices Die," consisting of two four-line stanzas, is a couplet rather than a quatrain poem.

The iambic pentameter couplet, first used by Chaucer in the *Canterbury Tales*, has been in continuous use since the fifteenth century. It was the verse form *de rigeur* in the late seventeenth and throughout most of the eighteenth centuries. All iambic pentameter couplets, whether "closed" or "open," are HEROIC COUPLETS, though Pope's preference for the closed couplet has accustomed us to think of it as the heroic. In an OPEN COUPLET (whether it be pentameter, tetrameter, or what not) the syntactical unit carries over into the first line of the next couplet, and there is no heavy pause at the end of its own second line:

> The sire then shook the honours of his head,
> And from his brows damps of oblivion shed
> Full on the filial dullness.

In a CLOSED COUPLET the syntactical unit comes to an end at the end of the second line, and there is a heavy pause or a full stop:

> Thoughtless as monarch oaks that shade the plain,
> And, spread in solemn state, supinely reign.

Used in various ways and contexts, couplets produce various effects: flowing, musical effects in Marlowe's "Hero and Leander"; wit and brilliance in Pope's "Rape of the Lock"; resonance and incantation in Shelley's "Music When Soft Voices Die." The couplet does, however, easily lend itself to wit and aphorism. The immediately juxtaposed rhymes make antithesis and witty elaboration quite effective, and the form is emphatic and highly mnemonic. At the conclusion of an English (Shakespearean) sonnet, the couplet is even more effective than usual as a climactic note and pithy conclusion; here the couplet has the effect of an emphatic variation from the normal pattern, since it has been preceded by twelve lines of *alternating* rhyme.

Many of our stanza forms are English adaptations of European models. The couplet was developed during the Anglo-Norman period (1066–1350). Closed couplets dominated the first half of the eighteenth century, open couplets the second. Jonathan Swift wrote a great many tetrameter or octosyllabic couplets; Dryden and Pope are the great masters of the heroic couplet. In the twentieth century, Roy Campbell, J. V. Cunningham, and Robert Frost have used couplet forms frequently and with genius.

EXAMPLES

tetrameter (octosyllabic)	HENRY VAUGHAN, *The World;* ROBERT BRIDGES, *Eros*
pentameter (open)	CHRISTOPHER MARLOWE, *Hero and Leander;* WILLIAM WORDSWORTH, *An Evening Walk*
pentameter (closed)	ALEXANDER POPE, *The Rape of the Lock;* SAMUEL JOHNSON, *The Vanity of Human Wishes*

II.   TERCETS

Three lines rhyming consecutively, or three-line stanzas of interlocking rhyme, are called TERCETS. When the three lines rhyme consecutively, the stanza is traditionally called a TRIPLET; in the other case *terza rima*. An unrhymed stanza of three lines (rare) is called a TRISTICH.

Terza rima
Thou who didst waken from his summer-dreams *a*
The blue Mediterranean, where he lay, *b*   *a*
Lull'd by the coil of his crystalline streams,

Beside a pumice isle in Baiae's bay, *a*
And saw in sleep old palaces and towers *b*
Quivering within the wave's intenser day. *a*

Triplet
Such sharpness shows the sweetest friend,
Such cuttings rather heal than rend,
And such beginnings touch their end.

Tercets are most frequent in the form of *terza rima*, which was introduced into English poetry, from the Italian, by Sir Thomas Wyatt early in the sixteenth century. Dante's *Divine Comedy* (*La Divina Commedia*) is the world's most famous *terza rima* poem. Since the rhyme scheme is fulfilled only as one moves from stanza to stanza, it pulls the attention, by pulling the ear, continuously forward. And because of this strong sense of forward movement, *terza rima* is equally well suited to narration or to description that seeks to create a unified or dominant impression.

Triplets are relatively rare in English, and there are no first-rate triplet poems of any considerable length. It is difficult to find sufficient rhyme, and difficult to endure such intense rhyming for more than a few stanzas. The Augustan poets sometimes allowed triplets in their heroic couplet poems, especially when an effect of expansion or intensification was desired. Robert Bridges' octosyllabic couplet poem "Eros" ends with a triplet that is strikingly effective by contrast.

EXAMPLES

terza rima	SHELLEY, *Ode to the West Wind;* BROWNING, *The Statue and the Bust*
triplets	GEORGE HERBERT, *Paradise;* ROBERT HERRICK, *Upon Julia's Clothes*

III.   QUATRAINS

The favorite English verse form is the quatrain, a stanza of four lines. Eight types of quatrains are fairly common: (1) the ballad stanza, (2) the long ballad, (3) the short ballad, (4) the heroic quatrain, (5) the *Rubaiyat* stanza, (6) the *In Memoriam* stanza, (7) the brace stanza, and (8) the unrhymed quatrain (often called a tetrastich). Ordinarily all of these are iambic, but trochaic quatrains are not rare, and traditionally the three ballad stanzas freely admit anapests and other types of feet.

There is nothing mysterious about the popularity of quatrains. Where the rhyme is alternating, they can be constructed as a two-part structure, making balance, parallelism, and antithesis quite feasible. And they save rhyme in a rhyme-poor language. When a relatively short and self-contained stanza is required, the quatrain is ready to hand. The interweaving, forward-pulling effects of *terza rima* rule out that form, and the tercet and the five-line stanza provide little opportunity for balance and antithesis. The five-line stanza (e.g., *ababa; abbab; ababb*) raises the problem of finding three identical rhymes, and so of course does the triplet, which has the additional disadvantage that it tends to cloy. Following are some quatrain patterns.

1.   Ballad Stanza

Lines 1 and 3 are iambic tetrameter, 2 and 4 trimeter; rhyme schemes *abab* or *xaxa*.

A slumber did my spirit seal;	*a*
I had no human fears;	*b*
She seemed a thing that could not feel	*a*
The touch of earthly years.	*b*

∾

There lived a wife at Usher's well,	*x*
And a wealthy wife was she;	*a*
She had three stout and stalwart sons,	*x*
And sent them o'er the sea.	*a*

2.   Long Ballad

All four lines are iambic tetrameter; rhyme schemes *abab, xaxa,* or *aabb*.

Bring me my bow of burning gold!	*a*
Bring me my arrows of desire!	*b*
Bring me my spear! O clouds, unfold!	*a*
Bring me my chariot of fire!	*b*

Blake "And Did Those Feet"

∾

Mock on, mock on, Voltaire, Rousseau,	*x*
Mock on, mock on; 'tis all in vain;	*a*
You throw the sand against the wind	*x*
And the wind blows it back again.	*a*

∾

What would the world be, once bereft	*a*
Of wet and wildness? Let them be left,	*a*
O let them be left, wildness and wet;	*b*
Long live the weeds and the wilderness yet.	*b*

3.   *Short Ballad*

Lines 1, 2, and 4 are iambic trimeter, line 3 tetrameter; rhyme scheme usually *xaxa*.

My girl, thou gazest much	*x*
Upon the golden skies:	*a*
Would I were heaven! I would behold	*x*
Thee then with all mine eyes!	*a*

4.   *Heroic Quatrain*

All four lines are iambic pentameter rhyming *abab*.

Not for a moment could I now behold	*a*
A smiling sea, and be what I have been:	*b*
The feeling of my loss will ne'er be old;	*a*
This, which I know, I speak with mind serene.	*b*

5.   *Rubaiyat Stanza*

The four lines are iambic pentameter rhyming *aaxa*.

They say the Lion and the Lizard keep	*a*
The courts where Jamshyd gloried and drank deep:	*a*
And Bahram, that great Hunter—the Wild Ass	*x*
Stamps o'er his Head, but cannot break his Sleep.	*a*

6.   *In Memoriam Stanza*

The four lines are iambic tetrameter rhyming *abba*.

So runs my dream: but what am I?	*a*
An infant crying in the night:	*b*
An infant crying for the light:	*b*
And with no language but a cry.	*a*

7.   *Brace Stanza*

All four lines are iambic pentameter rhyming *abba*. The first eight lines (the O C T A V E) of an Italian sonnet form two brace stanzas. The form is rare outside the sonnet.

Lawrence, of virtuous father virtuous son,   *a*
   Now that the fields are dank, and ways are mire,   *b*
   Where shall we sometimes meet, and by the fire   *b*
Help waste a sullen day; what may be won   *a*

From the hard season gaining: time will run   *a*
   On smoother, till Favonius reinspire   *b*
   The frozen earth; and clothe in fresh attire   *b*
The lily and the rose, that neither sowed nor spun.   *a*

8. *Unrhymed Quatrain (Tetrastich)*

This includes any unrhymed four-line stanza.

Now droops the milkwhite peacock like a ghost,   *x*
And like a ghost she glimmers on to me.   *x*
Now lies the earth all Danae to the stars,   *x*
And all thy heart lies open unto me.   *x*

As might be expected, trimeter, dimeter, and monometer quatrains are rarer than the eight types noted above. Even so, dimeters and trimeters crop up with fair frequency, especially in the work of the minor Elizabethan poets. Here is the first stanza of a dimeter quatrain poem by Wyatt:

With serving still
   This have I won,
For my goodwill
   To be undone.

Trochaic quatrains are almost always tetrameter and rhymed consecutively (*aabb*). William Blake and William Butler Yeats are masters of this form:

Tyger! Tyger! burning bright
In the forests of the night,
What immortal hand or eye
Could frame thy fearful symmetry.

The last line of Blake's stanza above is *iambic* tetrameter; iambic substitutions are common in this form. We noticed them earlier in Shelley's "Music When Soft Voices Die."

Of the eight common types of quatrains, the *Rubaiyat* stanza and the unrhymed quatrain are the rarest. The former taxes an English poet's rhyme capacity too hard, and the latter is unpopular for the simple reason that rhyme of some sort seems natural and desirable in lyric poetry. The short ballad—and of course regular trimeter, dimeter, and monometer quatrains as well—is also relatively rare because the line is too short for a normal breath; it tends to become mechanical because of the necessity of starting and stopping in such short intervals.

IV.   CINQUAINS

Cinquains (sǐng'kāns), five-line stanzas, are far less common than quatrains. Only one—the colloquial, highly popular, and highly anonymous limerick—has been formally christened.

1.   The Limerick

Lines 1, 2, and 5 are anapestic trimeter, 3 and 4 anapestic dimeter; rhyme scheme *aabba*. The verse is usually logaoedic, and sometimes quite irregular. The speed of the anapests and the shortness of the lines create a light and swinging effect that make this form well suited to wit and lighthearted moods. In the following limerick by Edward Lear, lines 3 and 4 have been combined:

> There was a young man from Iowa
> Who exclaimed, "Where on earth shall I stow her!"
> Of his sister he spoke, who was felled by an Oak
>   Which abound in the plains of Iowa.

2.   Unrhymed Cinquains

These are sometimes called pentastichs; here is the first stanza of one of Tennyson's songs from *The Princess:*

> Tears, idle tears, I know not what they mean,
> Tears from the depth of some divine despair
> Rise in the heart, and gather to the eyes,

In looking on the happy Autumn-fields,
And thinking of the days that are no more.

3.   Other Cinquains

There is great variety in pattern of line lengths and in rhyme scheme. The most common rhyme scheme, however, is *ababb:*

Helen, thy beauty is to me
  Like those Nicean barks of yore
That gently o'er a perfumed sea
  The weary, way-worn wanderer bore
To his own native shore.

V.   SIXAINS

Stanzas of six lines are more abundant than cinquains. Two of them are known by conventional names: the STAVE OF SIX and the SESTINA.

The stave of six is an iambic pentameter or tetrameter stanza rhyming *ababcc:*

Through Alpine meadows soft-suffused
With rain, where thick the crocus blows,
Past the dark forges long disused,
The mule-track from Saint Laurent goes.
The bridge is cross'd, and slow we ride,
Through forest, up the mountain-side.

The structure is that of a quatrain plus a couplet. Rarely, however, is the couplet used as an aphoristic or interpretive unit: four lines will not normally provide enough space for building up an argument or situation impressive enough to warrant the impressive couplet, and so the last two lines of the stave usually continue the particularity or argument of the first four. The stave of six seems to be useful when a poet is working in larger units of thought or description than are feasible in the quatrain. The stave has the advantage over a pattern such as *ababab* of requiring only a single pair of rhymes in each case. The stave was one of Matthew Arnold's favorite stanzas; the best known poem in the form, however, is undoubtedly Wordsworth's "I Wandered Lonely as a Cloud."

The sestina, a pattern of stanzas rather than a single-stanza pattern, is an elaborate and unlikely form that has remained rare in English for two reasons: it is difficult to manage, and it is suitable to a certain kind of expression only.

The English sestina consists of six six-line pentameter (or, more often, iambic hendecasyllabic) stanzas that repeat, each in a different and predetermined pattern, the end words of the lines of the first stanza. Here are two stanzas of Sir Philip Sidney's "Double Sestine":

> For she, whose parts maintained a perfect music,
> Whose beauty shined more than the blushing morning,
> Who much did pass in state the stately mountains,
> In straightness passed the cedars of the forests,
> Hath cast me wretch into eternal evening,
> By taking her two suns from these dark valleys.
>
> For she, to whom compared, the Alps are valleys,
> She, whose least word brings from the spheres their music,
> At whose approach the sun rose in the evening,
> Who, where she went, bare in her forehead morning,
> Is gone, is gone from these our spoiled forests,
> Turning to deserts our best pastured mountains.

Notice the main effect of the sestina: six words in already emphatic positions (at the ends of lines) are repeated six times, once in each of the six stanzas of the poem. The result is an enormous emphasis upon those words. The sestina seems not necessarily to be a mere curious exercise or virtuoso showpiece, but at least ideally to be a form designed to encourage and express a meditation or reverie upon certain thoughts or images. If such an obsessive vision or reverie-like impulse does not in fact exist or come into existence as the poem is written, the six key words will seem unmotivated and the whole poem will turn out to be an academic exercise. The sestina would seem to require the poet's deepest love and conviction, involve his deepest impressions as these take on a rather obsessive quality—if the poem is to offer us more than the pleasures of contrivance.

VI. THE SEVEN-LINE (SEPTET) STANZA

The RHYME ROYAL or CHAUCERIAN STANZA, a seven-line pentameter stanza rhyming *ababbcc*, is the only seven-line form at all familiar in English:

> Then, when confusion in her course shall bring
> Sad desolation on the times to come,
> When mirthless Thames shall have no swan to sing,
> All music silent, and the Muses dumb,
> And yet even then it must be known to some
> That once they flourished, though not cherished so,
> And Thames had swans as well as ever Po.

Rhyme royals having a hexameter seventh line are not uncommon: the induction to Milton's "Ode on the Morning of Christ's Nativity" and Wordsworth's "Resolution and Independence," for example.

The seven-line stanza has sufficient length to make it suitable for narrative poetry, and Chaucer, who introduced the form (borrowing it from the French), used it for his *Troilus and Criseyde*, a long romance which would make Middle English well worth learning even if we weren't invited to learn it by his *Canterbury Tales*. The couplet which concludes the stanza satisfies our desire to reach the resolution of a rhyme scheme, and so gives us a momentary rest, which is desirable in a long narrative poem. The nine-line Spenserian stanza, which also ends in a couplet, has the same advantage. Notice that the fifth line of the rhyme royal—the unexpected appearance of the *b*-rhyme—makes us all the more grateful for the following couplet.

VII. THE EIGHT-LINE (OCTAVE) STANZA

Octave stanzas are much more common than stanzas of five and seven lines. Quatrains are so familiar and so easy to manage in our language that an octave, which may be, and often is, essentially two joined quatrains, presents no very great difficulties.

Tetrameter octaves are almost as common as pentameter, but of them only the TRIOLET has a formal designation (though triolet lines may be longer or shorter than tetrameter; there is no "law").

The triolet rhymes *abaaabab*, and lines 1, 4, and 7 are identical, as
are lines 2 and 8:

> When first we met we did not guess ⌒
> That Love would prove so hard a master; ♭
> Of more than common friendliness ⌐
> When first we met we did not guess. ⌐
> Who could foretell this sore distress, ⌐
> This irretrievable disaster ♭
> When first we met?—We did not guess ⌐
> That Love would prove so hard a master. ♭

This verse form, like the sestina, is a special purpose stanza. It is
almost impossible to manage so much repetition in so short a space
without seeming playful, and of course such repetition makes the
form utterly unsuitable for narration or even for the most serious
lyrical expression. The triolet is for charm, not for passion. The
Bridges example above is one of the finest in the language; its mature
blending of playfulness and pathos is irresistible.

The COMMON OCTAVE is simply two pentameter or tetrameter quatrains joined. The rhyme may be *ababcdcd* or *xaxaxbxb:*

> Alone, as if enduring to the end
> A valiant armor of scarred hopes outworn,
> He stood there in the middle of the road
> Like Roland's ghost winding a silent horn.
> Below him, in the town among the trees,
> Where friends of other days had honored him,
> A phantom salutation of the dead
> Rang thinly till old Eben's eyes were dim.

The BRACE OCTAVE is any type of octave in which brace
rhyme (*abba*) is used; the pattern may be *abbaabba* or *abbacddc*. Yeats
wrote a number of poems in brace octaves; here is one of his tetrameter brace stanzas, the final one in "Two Songs from a Play":

> Everything that man esteems
> Endures a moment or a day.
> Love's pleasure drives his love away,
> The painter's brush consumes his dreams;

The herald's cry, the soldier's tread
Exhaust his glory and his might:
Whatever flames upon the night
Man's own resinous heart has fed.

The OTTAVA RIMA is the most common of English oc-
taves, although relatively speaking it is not a familiar stanza. The
lines are iambic pentameter and rhyme *abababcc*. An interesting and
flexible stanza, the ottava is the national or heroic stanza of Italy, where
it was developed. Many Italian epics and romances are written in
this form, and it was a favorite of Ariosto, Tasso, and Boccaccio—it
is sometimes called the Ariosto stanza. It was introduced into English
by Wyatt. Here is one of his epigram-like ottavas:

A face that should content me wondrous well
Should not be fair, but lovely to behold,
With gladsome cheer, all grief for to expel;
With sober looks, so would I that it should
Speak without words such words as none can tell;
The tress also should be of crisped gold.
With wit, and these, might chance I might be tied,
And knit again the knot that should not slide.

Byron was partial to the ottava, and his long, racy, digressive narrative *Don Juan* is still the best-known English ottava poem. Shelley
also liked the stanza, but his ottava poems are short and not among
his better-known pieces (some of them are fragments). In recent
times, Yeats took up the form, and a number of his best and most
famous poems are ottava rimas ("Sailing to Byzantium," "Among
School Children," "The Municipal Gallery Revisited").

The ottava seems to be about equally well suited to lyric and
narrative poetry, to serious and light work. Byron's stanzas in *Don
Juan* are often gay or witty; the lines become irregular to the point
of suggesting speech rhythms, and the rhymes are frequently feminine
for lightness and highly inventive and surprising. Many of Yeats's
ottava rima poems render just the opposite effects: high seriousness,
meditation, austerity.

The stanza is long enough to allow good elbowroom; it has
the space for solid development of a single theme, for detailed descrip-

tion, or for a significant advance in narration. And it is long enough that the closing couplet may—but need not—be used to good effect as an aphoristic comment deriving from the matter in the first six lines. The repeated rhymes create a certain acoustic intensity which will complement serious lyricism. The difficulty of the ottava, and probably the reason for its never having gotten into wide use in English, is the difficulty of finding so many suitable rhymes. Yeats solved this problem by freely admitting slant rhyme.

VIII. THE SPENSERIAN STANZA

For his long allegory *The Faerie Queene*, Edmund Spenser invented a unique stanza: nine lines rhyming *ababbcbcc*, the first eight lines of which are pentameter and the ninth hexameter. Subsequently the Spenserian stanza has appealed to a good many poets; Keats's "Eve of St. Agnes" is possibly the finest modern poem in the form; Shelley's "Adonais" and Burns's "The Cottager's Saturday Night" are other famous poems in the Spenserian. Here is the twenty-fifth stanza of "The Eve of St. Agnes":

> Full on this casement shone the wintry moon,
> And threw warm gules on Madeline's fair breast,
> As down she knelt for Heaven's grace and boon;
> Rose-bloom fell on her hands, together prest,
> And on her silver cross soft amethyst,
> And on her hair a glory, like a saint:
> She seemed a splendid angel, newly drest,
> Save wings, for heaven:—Porphyro grew faint:
> She knelt, so pure a thing, so free from mortal taint.

The great space of the stanza makes it well suited to detailed narration and description. It is so constructed as to bring the mind, and breath, almost to fatigue and then to force a rest before one goes on to the following stanza. This rest is necessitated by the length of the stanza—it is almost the largest stanza the mind can grasp as a whole—and by the extra effort of the closing hexameter line. The rest is prolonged by the acoustic satisfaction of the couplet formed by the eighth and ninth lines. These last two lines are rarely used, however, for aphorism or interpretation for two reasons: the stanza is normally used for description and narration, where there would be little call for pithy or ironic or synoptic comments at the ends of the stanzas; and the final two lines do not have quite the effect of a couplet since their *c*-rhyme has already been used in the sixth line and is retained in the memory. The "couplet" is not really a couplet; it tends to draw the mind back into the stanza, into the particulars of the narration or description, rather than to prepare it for a commenting or summarizing statement of some sort.

The special difficulties of the Spenserian are, first, the necessity of finding, again and again, four words of *b*- and three of *c*-rhyme, and second, the difficulty of shaping a thought or image of sufficient magnitude to make the extra length of the ninth line seem justified.

IX.   LONGER STANZAS

Stanzas of ten, eleven, or twelve lines are rarer than any of the shorter units, and not a single stanza of these lengths has a familiar name. Of the three, the ten-liner is easily the most common, and at once the best and the most widely known of these are the odes of Keats. His "Ode to Psyche" is a group of irregular stanzas, and his "Ode to Indolence" and "To Autumn" are in eleven-line stanzas; all of the others are in a "tenner" which rhymes (with the exception of two or three stanzas) *ababcdecde*. Here is the seventh stanza of his "Ode to a Nightingale":

> Thou wast not born for death, immortal bird!
>   No hungry generations tread thee down;
> The voice I hear this passing night was heard
>   In ancient days by emperor and clown:
> Perhaps the self-same song that found a path
>   Through the sad heart of Ruth, when, sick for home,
>   She stood in tears amid the alien corn;
>   The same that oft-times hath
>   Charmed magic casements, opening on the foam
>   Of perilous seas, in faery lands forlorn.

The longer a stanza becomes, the harder it is to feel and grasp as a unit. Stanzas longer than nine or ten lines—and often these too—tend to break up into smaller groups such as quatrains and cinquains.

X.   THE LONGER FRENCH FORMS: RONDEAU, RONDEL, VILLANELLE

All of these forms are rare and are quite variable in both stanza and line length. The villanelle is probably more common than the other two, and a few villanelles, such as Dylan Thomas's "Do Not Go Gentle into That Good Night," are serious and impressive poems; the rondel and rondeau are almost always light and playful.

The RONDEAU is typically thirteen lines running on only two rhymes; the first word or opening phrase of the first line is repeated as a refrain after the eighth and again after the thirteenth line. The most common stanzaic grouping is *aabba, aabR, aabbaR*. Wyatt introduced the form into English. Here is Austin Dobson's rondeau *With Pipe and Flute:*

> With pipe and flute the rustic Pan
> Of old made music sweet for man;
>   And wonder hushed the warbling bird,
>   And closer drew the calm-eyed herd,—
> The rolling river slowlier ran.
>
> Ah! would,—ah! would, a little span,
> Some air of Arcady could fan
>   This age of ours, too seldom stirred
>   With pipe and flute!
>
> But now for gold we plot and plan;
> And from Beersheba unto Dan
>   Apollo's self might pass unheard,
>   Or find the night-jar's note preferred,—
> Not so it fared when time began
>   With pipe and flute!

The RONDEL is usually a poem of fourteen lines running on two rhymes; the first two lines are exactly repeated as lines seven

and eight and again as lines thirteen and fourteen. But the pattern
is often varied. Here is a rondel by Dobson:

> Too hard it is to sing
>   In these untuneful times,
> When only coin can ring,
>   And no one cares for rhymes.
>   Alas for him who climbs
> To Aganippe's Spring:
> Too hard it is to sing
>   In these untuneful times.
>
> His kindred clip his wing,
>   His feet the critic limes;
> If fame her laurel bring,
>   Old age his forehead rimes:
> Too hard it is to sing
>   In these untuneful times.

Like the rondeau and rondel, the V I L L A N E L L E runs on only
two rhymes; typically it is of nineteen lines, but may be longer or
shorter. The first line is repeated as the sixth and twelfth lines, and
the third line is repeated as the ninth and fifteenth. Both the first and
third lines occur again in the final four lines. Villanelles are always
divided into tercets. This one is by Oscar Wilde:

> *Theocritus*
> O singer of Persephone!
>   In the dim meadows desolate
> Dost thou remember Sicily?
>
> Still through the ivy flits the bee
>   Where Amaryllis lies in state;
> O Singer of Persephone!
>
> Simaetha calls on Hecate
>   And hears the wild dogs at the gate:
> Dost thou remember Sicily?
>
> Still by the light and laughing sea
>   Poor Polypheme bemoans his fate;
> O Singer of Persephone!

And still in boyish rivalry
    Young Daphnis challenges his mate;
Dost thou remember Sicily?

Slim Lacon keeps a goat for thee,
    For thee the jocund shepherds wait;
O Singer of Persephone!
Dost thou remember Sicily?

All three of these forms pose a great problem: how is one to find so much rhyme, and incorporate so much repetition, without being merely ingenious? Many poems in these forms take as subject matter the form itself, and are consequently rather tiresome.

XI. THE ODES

It is difficult to say what an ode is. One is tempted to describe it as a poem of some length which does not follow any of the other conventional forms. Some poems which poets have titled odes follow a fixed or nearly fixed stanzaic pattern, for example all of the Keats odes except the "Ode to Psyche." These it is convenient to call STANZAIC odes. Other odes, however, are extremely free, are unpredictable in everything—stanza length, line length, meter, and rhyme pattern. Most odes rhyme in some fashion, and nearly all of them are either highly formal or elaborate. Praise and commemoration are frequent motives; personification and direct address are characteristic of the rhetoric.

Stanzaic Odes

As we have already indicated, any poem that a poet cares to call an ode can scarcely be challenged as not being sufficiently odic. Of those odes that follow a regular, or nearly regular, stanzaic pattern, the HORATIAN ode (so called because it is patterned after the odes of Horace [Rome, 65–8 B.C.]) is the only one that has both been used by a number of poets and gotten a name.

'The Horatian may be rhymed (*aabb*) or unrhymed; in any case it is a quatrain in which the first two lines are longer than the third and fourth. Below are some stanzas from the two best-known English poems in the form; the first stanza is from Andrew Marvell's "On Cromwell's Return," the second from William Collins' unrhymed "Ode to Evening":

He nothing common did, or mean,
Upon that memorable scene,
    But with his keener eye
    The axe's edge did try.

∾

If aught of oaten stop, or pastoral song,
May hope, chaste Eve, to soothe thy modest ear,
    Like thy own solemn springs,
    Thy springs, and dying gales,
O Nymph reserved, while now the bright-haired sun
Sits in yon western tent, whose cloudy skirts,
    With brede ethereal wove,
    O'erhang his wavy bed.

Pindaric Ode

This is an extraordinarily elaborate form, derived originally from the odes of Pindarus (Athens, d. 443 B.C.). In some respects the Pindaric ode is a fixed form, in others it is open to the poet's invention. It consists of three stanzas called, respectively, the "strophe" or "turn," the "antistrophe" or "counterturn," and the "epode" or "stand." The first two of these stanzas are identical in pattern except for the rhyme sounds, but the form itself is up to the poet. The third stanza is almost different in form from the other two. Taken together, the three stanzas form a SECTION, and a Pindaric ode may consist of any number of sections.

The Greek chorus chanted the strophe as they moved across the stage, the antistrophe as they returned to their original position, and the epode as they then stood in the original position.

Here is Ben Jonson's Pindaric ode to Cary and Morison:

strophe
It is not growing like a tree
In bulk, doth make men better be;
Or standing long an oak, three hundred year,
To fall a log at last, dry, bald, and sere:
     A lily of a day,
     Is fairer far, in May,
   Although it fall and die that night;
   It was the plant and flower of light.
In small proportions we just beauties see;
And in short measures life may perfect be.

antistrophe
Call, noble Lucius, then, for wine,
And let thy looks with gladness shine;
Accept this garland, plant it on thy head,
And think, nay know, thy Morison's now dead.
     He leaped the present age,
     Possest with holy rage,
   To see that bright eternal day;
   Of which we priests and poets say
Such truths as we expect for happy men;
And there he lives with memory and Ben

epode
Jonson, who sung this of him, ere he went,
     Himself to rest,
Or taste a part of that full joy he meant
     To have exprest,
     In this bright asterism;
     Where it were friendship's schism,
  Were not his Lucius long with us to tarry,
     To separate these twi-
     Lights, the Dioscuri,
  And keep the one half from his Harry.
But fate doth so alternate the design,
Whilst that in heaven, this light on earth must shine.

Cowleian Ode

This, the freest of all metrical forms, is named after Abraham
Cowley (London, 1618–1667). The only thing two Cowleian odes

will have in common is that both will use rhyme and meter in some fashion. Everything else is indeterminate. Here are the first three stanzas of the finest such ode in English, Wordsworth's "Intimations of Immortality":

> There was a time when meadow, grove, and stream,
>   The earth, and every common sight,
>   To me did seem
>   Apparelled in celestial light,
> The glory and the freshness of a dream.
> It is not now as it hath been of yore;—
>   Turn wheresoe'er I may,
>   By night or day,
> The things which I have seen I now can see no more.
>
>   The Rainbow comes and goes,
>   And lovely is the Rose,
>   The Moon doth with delight
>   Look round her when the heavens are bare,
>   Waters on a starry night
>   Are beautiful and fair;
>   The sunshine is a glorious birth;
>   But yet I know, where'er I go,
> That there hath past away a glory from the earth.
>
> Now, while the birds thus sing a joyous song,
>   And while the young lambs bound
>   As to the tabor's sound,
> To me alone there came a thought of grief:
> A timely utterance gave that thought relief,
>   And I again am strong:
> The cataracts blow their trumpets from the steep;
> No more shall grief of mine the season wrong;
> I hear the Echoes through the mountains throng,
> The Winds come to me from the fields of sleep,
>   And all the earth is gay;
>   Land and sea
>   Give themselves up to jollity,
>   And with the heart of May
>   Doth every beast keep holiday;—
>   Thou Child of Joy,
> Shout round me, let me hear thy shouts, thou happy Shepherd-boy!

XII.   RARE STANZAS: SEGUIDILLA, RONDELET, BALLADE, ROUNDEL, HAIKU, TANKA

The SEGUIDILLA, a Spanish form, is most often a four- or seven-line stanza. There is as yet no agreement on just what an English seguidilla should be. Most of those that have appeared as original English poems show a pattern of varying line lengths, and there is some kind of rhyme scheme. Here is an excellent one called simply "Seguidilla" by Richard Wirtz Emerson:

> Our love is like soft rain
>   washing away
> each dry vestige of shame
>   left by the day
>   in its retreat
> from the hours which lay
>   dead at our feet.

The RONDELET is a five- or seven-line stanza running on two rhymes and using the opening phrase of the first line as a refrain. It is extremely rare in English.

The BALLADE, another Gallic importation, consists of three stanzas and a four-line ENVOY (a kind of conclusion or dedicatory stanza). The ballade uses three rhymes, and each stanza uses the same rhyme sounds; the scheme is *ababbcbc*. The last line of the first stanza is used as the last line of the other two stanzas and of the envoy. The excessive repetition of rhyme sounds will keep this form one of the least likely ones for English poets. There are variants of the ballade form, the most notorious of them being the CHANT ROYAL, which is perhaps the most difficult and elaborate verse form ever devised in a modern European language. Here is Austin Dobson's "Ballad of Imitation":

> If they hint, O Musician, the piece that you played
>   Is nought but a copy of Chopin or Spohr;
> That the ballad you sing is but merely "conveyed"
>   From the stock of the Arnes and the Purcells of yore;
>   That there's nothing, in short, in the words or the score

That is not as out-worn as the "Wandering Jew,"
  Make answer—Beethoven could scarcely do more—
That the man who plants cabbages imitates, too!

If they tell you, Sir Artist, your light and your shade
  Are simply "adapted" from other men's lore;
That—plainly to speak of a "spade" as a "spade"—
  You've "stolen" your grouping from three or from four;
  That (however the writer the truth may deplore),
'Twas Gainsborough painted *your* "Little Boy Blue";
  Smile only serenely—though cut to the core—
For the man who plants cabbages imitates, too!

And you too, my Poet, be never dismayed
  If they whisper your Epic—"Sir Éperon d'Or"—
Is nothing but Tennyson thinly arrayed
  In a tissue that's taken from Morris's store;
  That no one, in fact, but a child could ignore
That you "lift" or "accommodate" all that you do;
  Take heart—though your Pegasus' withers be sore—
For the man who plants cabbages imitates, too!

Postscriptum—And you, whom we all so adore,
  Dear Critics, whose verdicts are always so new!—
One word in your ear. There were Critics before . . .
  And the man who plants cabbages imitates, too!

The ROUNDEL is a French-inspired form devised by Swinburne. It is an eleven-line stanza running on two rhymes: *abax bab
abax*. The opening phrase is used as a refrain. The form has had few
takers.

The HAIKU or HOKKU and the TANKA are not stanza or
section forms, but merely verses composed of a predetermined
number of syllables: seventeen in the former, thirty-one in the latter.
Both forms are Japanese.

XIII. RHYMELESS STANZAS

Occasionally poets have used rhymeless stanzas. We have
already noticed some examples: Tennyson's song "Tears, Idle Tears"

in five-line stanzas, and Collins' unrhymed "Ode to Evening." Rhymeless stanzas may, of course, take any form whatsoever.

The relative unpopularity of the rhymeless lyric is sufficiently explained by the fact that we miss the melodic and architectural qualities of rhyme—and we miss the rhyme all the more because our ears have been led to expect it in lyric poems. A poem, no matter how self-sufficient, is never read and experienced in a vacuum.

14
The Sonnet

Poems consisting of only a single stanza are not at all uncommon, and among them are some of the finest short poems in English. But the limitations of such brevity are obvious. A poem of one stanza cannot be much more than an epigram or a single lyric cry. The fourteen lines of the sonnet, however, offer room for the full development of a single, but perhaps impressively subtle, imaginative, and complete idea. A sonnet is large enough to allow the poet to set forth a problem and then go on to solve it (or find it insoluble); to present a situation and then interpret it; to move in one direction and then to reverse that direction completely. As we know them today, the two chief sonnet forms—the Italian and the English—are rather artificial, which does not mean they are necessarily "pretentious" or "false to experience," but that they are highly formal and rather arbitrary in structure. And yet if they were not in existence, almost certainly some other form or forms of about fourteen lines of rhyming iambic pentameter would have become equally famous: a form capable of giving a single idea or a single aspect of experience vivid definition in a single verse paragraph is obviously logical and desirable.

It is surprisingly difficult to make an unexceptionable definition of the form. Normally, of course, the sonnet is fourteen lines of iambic pentameter rhyming in some alternating fashion. But there have been sonnets longer than fourteen lines (there is an eighteen-line sonnet in *Romeo and Juliet*, I,v) and there are tetrameter and hexameter sonnets. The Elizabethans, in fact, gave out the sonnet title indiscriminately; the word's etymology, after all (Italian *sonetto* and Provençal *sonet*), meant "little song." It is possible to make a quite narrow definition: some writers have insisted, for example, that merely to call a fourteen-line rhyming iambic pentameter poem a sonnet is not necessarily to make it a sonnet. They have pointed out that fourteen iambic pentameter lines of predominantly *alternating* rhyme act upon the sensibility in a different and somehow nobler way than any variant of this pattern. A more catholic definition, however, is perfectly defensible, and avoids more difficulties than it raises.

Wyatt wrote our first sonnets. His model usually was the PETRARCHAN SONNET (Francesco Petrarch, 1304–1374; two books of sonnets inspired by Laura, a noble lady: *Sonnetto in Vita, Sonnetto in Morte*—sonnets written for the living, and for the dead, Laura). Wyatt's sonnets, unlike Petrarch's usually end in a couplet, and the iambic meter, like that in many of Wyatt's other poems, is often rough—whether deliberately or inadvertently, no one knows:

> Whoso list to hunt, I know where is an hind,
> But as for me—alas, I may no more.
> The vain travail hath wearied me so sore,
> I am of them that farthest cometh behind.
> Yet may I, by no means, my wearied mind
> Draw from the deer; but as she fleeth afore,
> Fainting I follow. I leave off therefore,
> Since in a net I seek to hold the wind.
> Who list her hunt, I put him out of doubt,
> As well as I, may spend his time in vain.
> And graven with diamonds in letters plain
> There is written, her fair neck round about:
> *Noli me tangere*, for Caesar's I am,
> And wild for to hold, though I seem tame.

⟩The ITALIAN SONNET is a two-part form: the first eight lines form the OCTAVE, and the last six the SESTET. The rhyme scheme of the octave is always *abbaabba;* the scheme of the sestet varies but is most often *cdecde* or *cdcdcd.* The sestet is not supposed to end with a couplet, but one finds the couplet ending in many sonnets otherwise Italian in form—as in the Wyatt sonnet above. Here is a sonnet by Robert Bridges (*The Growth of Love*, 33) that follows the Italian pattern perfectly:

> I care not if I live, tho' life and breath
> Have never been to me so dear and sweet.
> I care not if I die, for I could meet—
> Being so happy—happily my death.
> I care not if I love; to-day she saith
> She loveth, and love's history is complete.
> Nor care I if she love me; at her feet
> My spirit bows entranced and worshippeth.
>
> I have no care for what was most my care,
> But all around me see fresh beauty born,
> And common sights grown lovelier than they were:
> I dream of love, and in the light of morn
> Tremble, beholding all things very fair
> And strong with strength that puts my strength to scorn.

Bridges was able to complete his sonnet cycle only by abandoning the Italian form, whose demands for repeated rhymes proved too great an obstacle, in favor of the English (or Shakespearean) sonnet, a form developed by Wyatt's younger contemporary, Henry Howard, Earl of Surrey (1517–1547).

The two-part division invites a subject that may be developed in two parts. The octave presents a problem and the sestet solves it; or the octave may express one desire or vision, the sestet a conflicting one. Many of John Donne's Holy Sonnets—which are Italian in form except for the concluding couplet—are little dramas in which the poet's will or ego first asserts itself and then seeks to bend itself to the Divine will:

If poisonous minerals, and if that tree
Whose fruit threw death on else immortal us,
If lecherous goats, if serpents envious
Cannot be damned, Alas! why should I be?
Why should intent or reason, born in me,
Make sins, else equal, in me more heinous?
And mercy being easy, and glorious
To God, in his stern wrath why threatens he?

But who am I, that dare dispute with thee,
O God? O! of thine only worthy blood,
And my tears, make a heavenly Lethean flood,
And drown in it my sin's black memory;
That thou remember them, some claim as debt,
I think it mercy, if thou wilt forget.

Such dramatic contrasts are made subtly more effective by the contrasting rhyme sounds in the two divisions.

English poets have struck a number of variations from the normal Italian pattern. Often, as we have already noticed, there is a couplet ending. Sometimes one of the rhyme sounds of the octave will be continued in the sestet. Sometimes there is no distinct division, or no division at all, into octave and sestet.

≻The ENGLISH or SHAKESPEAREAN SONNET is made of three heroic quatrains and a concluding couplet. The constantly changing and finally pairing rhyme creates an effect quite different from that of the sinuous, interweaving quality of the echoing rhyme of octave and alternating rhyme of sestet. Once again, theme tends to follow form, and so the three quatrains of the English sonnet typically present three aspects of an idea. This tripartite division is well illustrated in Shakespeare's Sonnet 73:

That time of year thou mayst in me behold
When yellow leaves, or none, or few, do hang
Upon those boughs which shake against the cold,
Bare ruin'd choirs, where late the sweet birds sang.
In me thou see'st the twilight of such day
As after sunset fadeth in the west;
Which by and by black night doth take away,
Death's second self, that seals up all in rest.

In me thou see'st the glowing of such fire,
That on the ashes of his youth doth lie,
As the death-bed whereon it must expire,
Consum'd with that which it was nourish'd by.
This thou perceiv'st, which makes thy love more strong,
To love that well which thou must leave ere long.

Here are three metaphors of decay and death: autumn tree, sunset, and dying fire. The final couplet makes explicit their poignant theme.

Edmund Spenser developed his own variant of the English form, known as the S P E N S E R I A N S O N N E T: *ababbcbccdcdee*. This scheme found no followers. The four *b*- and *c*-rhymes present the difficulty.

Sonnets have been popular in every century except the eighteenth, when they were crowded out by the theory and brilliant practice of the heroic couplet. They were especially popular in the Elizabethan age; Shakespeare, Spenser, Sidney, Daniel, Drayton, Fulke Greville, and many very minor poets wrote long sonnet cycles. Donne's Holy Sonnets are among the finest devotional poems, and some of Milton's sonnets are among the great short poems in English. After a Petrarchan beginning, Milton broke with that tradition, and wrote intensely personal sonnets, many of them occasional poems. Wordsworth was fired to write sonnets by the example of Milton's intensity and grandeur. Apparently he was also greatly attracted to the sonnet because it provided an opportunity—in writing, as in reading, one—for intense meditation. The sonnet's redeemed prestige in the Romantic age owes a great deal to Wordsworth's successes, and a great deal to the fact that it conjured up memories of a period—the Renaissance—greatly amenable to Romantic tastes. Much of Hopkins' best work is in his sonnets. Jones Very and Robert Frost are American masters of the form. Elizabeth Daryush was the first to write sonnets in syllabic verse.

THE SONNET WRITERS

The following table lists some of the more important sonnet writers, the sonnet groups for which they are best known, and the form they favored. *Variant* means that the form is not "pure" English or Italian.

Sir Thomas Wyatt (1503–1542)	miscellaneous	Italian (variant)
Earl of Surrey (1516–1547)	miscellaneous	English (some variant)
Edmund Spenser (1552–1599)	*Amoretti*	English (variant)
Sir Philip Sidney (1554–1586)	*Astrophel and Stella*	Italian (variant)
Fulke Greville (1554–1628)	*Caelica*	English (variant)
Samuel Daniel (1562–1619)	*Delia*	English
Michael Drayton (1563–1631)	*Idea*	English
William Shakespeare (1564–1616)	Sonnets	English
Ben Jonson (1572–1637)	miscellaneous	Italian and English
John Donne (1572–1631)	Holy Sonnets	Italian (variant)
John Milton (1608–1674)	miscellaneous	Italian (some variant)
William Wordsworth (1770–1850)	miscellaneous	Italian
John Keats (1795–1821)	miscellaneous	Italian and English
E. B. Browning (1806–1861)	*Sonnets from the Portuguese*	Italian
Matthew Arnold (1822–1888)	miscellaneous	Italian
Dante Gabriel Rossetti (1828–1882)	*The House of Life*	Italian
Gerard Manley Hopkins (1844–1889)	miscellaneous	Italian
Robert Bridges (1844–1930)	*The Growth of Love*	Italian and English
Elizabeth Daryush	miscellaneous	English (some variant), syllabic verse sonnets
Robert Frost (1875–1963)	miscellaneous	Variant

Edna St.Vincent Millay
Robert Lowell

15
Blank Verse

Earlier we examined a passage from Surrey's blank verse translation of a book of the *Aeneid*, and concluded that it was rather wooden. The pioneer work in any form is not likely to be the best. It was not long after Surrey, however, that blank verse—in the hands of Marlowe and Shakespeare—reached perfection. The blank verse of Marlowe's play *Tamburlaine* is already magnificent. Shakespeare made it a still more flexible medium. And so much great, excellent, and better-than-competent blank verse has been written since Surrey that it must be regarded as the characteristic form of longer English poems.

Blank verse is undoubtedly the easiest kind of verse to write. One does not have to search for rhymes or move them into the right places, and one does not have to worry about the confines of a stanza. To juxtapose words so that every other syllable receives a stress is not much of a problem. But because it *is* so easy, and because it is such a spare form, it is one of the hardest to *master*. The absence of rhyme and stanza form invites prolixity and diffuseness—so easy is it to wander on and on. And blank verse has to be handled in a skillful, ever-attentive way to compensate for such qualities as the musical, architectural, and emphatic properties of rhyme; for the sense of direction one feels within a well-turned stanza; and for the rests that come in stanzas. There are no helps. It is like going into a thick woods in unfamiliar acres.

THE BLANK VERSE WRITERS AND THEIR WORKS

The following table lists some of the more famous blank verse poems and plays. In cases where a poet has written a great body of blank verse (e.g., Shakespeare, Tennyson, Wordsworth) only a few representative titles are listed.

Marlowe	*Tamburlaine, Doctor Faustus*
Shakespeare	*Hamlet, The Tempest*
Jonson	*Volpone, Sejanus*
Ford	*The Broken Heart, 'Tis Pity She's a Whore*
Webster	*The White Devil, The Duchess of Malfi*
Milton	*Paradise Lost, Samson Agonistes* (in part)
Wordsworth	*The Prelude, Tintern Abbey*
Keats	*Hyperion*
Tennyson	*Ulysses, Idylls of the King*
Browning	*Andrea del Sarto, One Word More*
Arnold	*Sohrab and Rustum*
Yeats	*On Baile's Strand, The Second Coming*
Frost	*The Death of the Hired Man, Birches*
Stevens	*Sunday Morning*
Aiken	*Preludes to Attitude*
Hart Crane	*The Bridge* (in part)
Maxwell Anderson	*Key Largo, The Wingless Victory*
Fry	*A Sleep of Prisoners, The Lady's Not for Burning*

EXAMPLES

The following lines are from Marlowe's play *The Tragicall Historie of Doctor Faustus* (c. 1586). Faustus is speaking.

(i)   Yes, I will wound Achilles in the heel,
       And then return to Helen for a kiss.
       Oh, thou art fairer than the evening air
       Clad in the beauty of a thousand stars;
       Brighter art thou than flaming Jupiter
       When he appeared to hapless Semele;
       More lovely than the monarch of the sky
       In wanton Arethusa's azured arms;
       And none but thou shalt be my paramour!

Notice how regular the meter is: there are only seven or eight variations from iambic in the nine lines—less than one to a line. Yet the
passage is by no means stiff; it suggests actual speech, at an intoxicated level.

These famous lines, spoken by Theseus in *A Midsummer-
night's Dream*, an early Shakespeare comedy, show the playwright
taking certain liberties with the medium shaped for him by Marlowe.

(ii)   The poet's eye, in a fine frenzy rolling,
       Doth glance from heaven to earth, from earth to heaven;
       And, as imagination bodies forth
       The forms of things unknown, the poet's pen
       Turns them to shapes, and gives to airy nothing
       A local habitation and a name.

The lines are *looser* than Marlowe's. Notice that some are runover
lines, and notice the feminine endings. Marlowe's lines typically show
neither of these characteristics. And in these six lines there are as
many metrical variations as one finds in Marlowe's nine.

(iii) Our revels now are ended. These our actors,
       As I foretold you, were all spirits, and
       Are melted into air, into thin air;
       And, like the baseless fabric of this vision,
       The cloud-capped towers, the gorgeous palaces,
       The solemn temples, the great globe itself,
       Yea, all which it inherit, shall dissolve,
       And, like this insubstantial pageant faded,
       Leave not a rack behind.

This is from one of Prospero's speeches in *The Tempest*, Shakespeare's last play. Here we find still another liberty rare in Marlowe and fairly rare in Shakespeare's own earlier plays: the freedom to end a line on a light syllable such as *and* or the final syllable of *palaces*. Three of the eight lines also show feminine endings. And the pauses within the lines are more numerous and of more varied kinds than is characteristic of Marlowe's blank verse.

Here are the last lines of *Paradise Lost;* Adam and Eve are leaving The Garden.

(*iv*)   They looking back, all th' Eastern side beheld
       Of Paradise, so late thir happy seat,
       Wav'd over by that flaming Brand, the Gate
       With dreadful Faces throng'd and fiery Arms:
       Some natural tears they dropp'd, but wip'd them soon;
       The World was all before them, where to choose
       Thir place of rest, and Providence thir guide:
       They hand in hand with wand'ring steps and slow,
       Through *Eden* took thir solitary way.

Milton's blank verse is the strictest in English, and this passage, which shows very few deviations from pure iambic meter, is typical. Most writers of blank verse since Surrey and Marlowe have allowed themselves such liberties as occasional hexameters, inversions of three or more feet to a line, anapestic as well as trochaic, spondaic, and pyrrhic substitutions, feminine endings, and frequent runon lines. But variations from the theoretical pattern are very carefully controlled and sparsely employed in Milton's epics.

These are some of the chief metrical characteristics of *Paradise Lost* and of Milton's later poem *Paradise Regained:* (1) insistence on ten and only ten syllables to the line; (2) trochaic, spondaic, and pyrrhic (or "ionic") substitutions only; (3) reluctance to allow more than one substitution to a line; (4) even greater reluctance to allow the final (fifth) foot to be anything but an iamb; (5) a high percentage of runon lines; (6) few feminine endings; (7) freedom in the position of caesuras. Milton's tightly controlled verse rarely becomes monotonous, however, despite its self-imposed austerity. If his blank verse were looser, *Paradise Lost* would probably not be read at all.

(v)   So through the darkness and the cold we flew,
        And not a voice was idle; with the din
        Smitten, the precipices rang aloud;
        The leafless trees and every icy crag
        Tinkled like iron; while far distant hills
        Into the tumult sent an alien sound
        Of melancholy not unnoticed, while the stars
        Eastward were sparkling clear, and in the west
        The orange sky of evening died away.

These lines, in which Wordsworth describes his boyhood ice-skating, are Wordsworthian blank verse at its best. The passage is markedly regular. Often, however, Wordsworth allows great liberties in his blank verse; a characteristic weakness is the absence of four or five strong stresses in the line—the verse becomes flaccid. Feminine endings are rare.

(vi)   The pungent oranges and bright, green wings
        Seem things in some procession of the dead,
        Winding across wide water, without sound.
        The day is like wide water, without sound,
        Stilled for the passing of her dreaming feet
        Over the seas, to silent Palestine,
        Dominion of the blood and sepulchre.

This is from Wallace Stevens' "Sunday Morning." The tenor is modern but the meter might be that of Marlowe or John Ford. Stevens' is the most impressive blank verse of the twentieth century.

WEBSTERIAN VERSE

Very loose blank verse has come to be called Websterian verse. In John Webster's two plays *The White Devil* and *The Duchess of Malfi* the blank verse frequently becomes almost free verse or prose:

        But for their sister, the right noble duchess,
        You never fixed your eye on three fair medals
        Cast in one figure, of so different temper.
        For her discourse, it is so full of rapture
        You only will begin then to be sorry
        When she doth end her speech, and wish, in wonder . . .

&

> Will you make yourself a mercenary herald,
> Rather to examine men's pedigrees, than virtues?
> You shall want him:
> For know an honest statesman to a prince,
> Is like a cedar planted by a spring:
> The spring bathes the tree's root, the grateful tree
> Rewards it with his shadow—you have not done so.

The first passage is fairly regular except that all the lines have feminine endings. The second passage is scarcely iambic at all except for the fourth and fifth lines. Some of T. S. Eliot's poetry is properly described as Websterian verse. Here are the opening lines of "Gerontion":

> Here I am, an old man in a dry month,
> Being read to by a boy, waiting for rain.
> I was neither at the hot gates
> Nor fought in the warm rain
> Nor knee deep in the salt marsh, heaving a cutlass,
> Bitten by flies, fought.

The blank verse of Maxwell Anderson's verse plays is often of the Websterian kind:

> It doesn't come to us at all. It comes to many
> in certain generations, comes to only a few
> in others; and it says, if you want to live
> you must die now—this instant—or the food
> you eat will rot at your lips, and the lips you kiss
> will turn to stone.

Matthew Arnold's "Philomela" is Websterian verse rather than free verse, as it is sometimes mistakenly described. The meter is iambic in almost every line:

> Dost thou tonight behold,
> Here, through the moonlight on this English grass,
> The unfriendly palace in the Thracian wild?
> Dost thou again peruse
> With hot cheeks and sear'd eyes
> The too clear web, and thy dumb sister's shame?

COMMON METRICAL VARIATIONS

In blank verse—and generally in iambic pentameter verse, whether rhymed or unrhymed—most of the major and better minor poets, from Spenser and Sidney to the present day, have written what may be described as a traditional pentameter; that is, they have tended to restrict their variations or licenses to four types, which may be codified as follows:

1. An ionic foot (; "Through the twelve tribes, | to rule | by laws | ordained") may substitute for any two successive iambic feet. Some writers prefer to think of the ionic as a pyrrhic followed by a spondee ("Through the | twelve tribes . . .").

2. Elision—the fusion or slurring (actual or theoretical) of two adjacent unstressed vowel sounds, or the theoretical exclusion of a weak vowel sound within a word—is possible at any available point:

By his prescript a sanctuary is framed;   y *is elided with* i

Obedient to his will, that he vouchsafes.   i *is elided with* e

3. A line may have a feminine ending; the extra (eleventh) syllable is not regarded as making the line hendecasyllabic:

And if | she be | not mis|tress of | this na|ture.
  1   2 | 3   4 | 5   6 | 7   8 | 9   10|11

4. The last (fifth) foot is always iambic. The incidence of trochaic feet in the fifth foot is so small as to be negligible. An exception, pointed out by Robert Bridges, is Keats's line,

Bright star, would I were stedfast as thou art.

The effect is one of extraordinary emphasis. Such an emphasis is very seldom called for.

16
Free Verse

Because FREE VERSE is free to be regular as well as to be free, it is difficult to define. One is forced to define it by generalization and by example, rather than formally. It is poetry that is not regular enough to be called verse but that is free to use, at any given point, any of the techniques or devices of verse—including meter and rhyme. We have already noticed that Whitman employs assonance, alliteration, rhyme, and occasionally meter in his free verse poem "When Lilacs Last in the Dooryard Bloom'd." Good free verse is always more concentrated and almost always less direct than prose, and at its leanest it still employs at least one technical device that is a characteristic of poetry and not of prose—the line.

One can think of possible difficulties in describing free verse: Is a poem that is irregular in every way except that it consistently rhymes *abab* free verse? Is a poem that is without rhyme, stanza, formal devices of sound, and formal patterns of syllable count and line length, but that is written throughout in rapidly changing but distinct feet of various kinds (e.g., iambs, trochees, anapests) free verse? But it is more important to see the most typical characteristics of the best free verse than to worry about a strictly logical, unassailable definition.

A typical free verse poem shows no formal prosodic devices and is unrhymed throughout. It is as difficult to scan as prose; at least, no two persons' scansions will be at all the same. And yet it has form: the arrangement of syllables and words, the line lengths, and the distribution of pauses fit the sense at every point.

By now free verse is no longer the so-called experimental, controversial, revolutionary development it was thought to be in the late nineteenth and early twentieth century. The one work that was undoubtedly more important than any other in gaining international prestige for the new form was Whitman's book of free verse poems *Leaves of Grass* (first edition, 1855). Active and influential free verse schools arose in France and Germany and, some time later, in England. Richard Aldington, H. D., Amy Lowell, John Gould Fletcher, Ezra Pound, T. S. Eliot, D. H. Lawrence, and William Carlos Williams were some of the English and American poets most interested in the possibilities of the new meterless poetry. All of them—and of course many other poets, including even so conservative a writer as Robert Bridges—felt that traditional prosody was "exhausted" or nearly so, and that a new age demanded new forms.

Eliot suggested that the underlying metrical structure of the English language might no longer be the old iambic, but some new rhythmic principle brought about by changed diction and habits of speech and by the habituation of modern ears to such rhythms as those of the diesel engine. According to Harriet Monroe, free verse represented "a demand for greater freedom of movement within the bar and line," and Richard Aldington remarked that it forced one "to create his own rhythms instead of imitating other people's." Aldington was too optimistic: many poems, some of them good, some of them quite bad, have been written in imitation of the free verse of Ezra Pound, T. S. Eliot, and William Carlos Williams. And of course many dilettantes, and a few earnest but mistaken zealots, welcomed the free verse movement as an escape from discipline and an excuse for linguistic anarchy and incompetence. Edith Sitwell has pointed out that the advent of free verse opened the floodgates for all those writers who thought that it would now be possible to chop passages of bad or indifferent prose into lines and pass off the insipid result as poetry. But of course the poseurs and otherwise untalented writers of conventional verse have always been legion too. Robert Bridges preferred to go no farther than syllabic verse, and T. S. Eliot was soon to remark that no good verse is really free. Eliot, Wallace Stevens, and others have written equally well in free and in more orthodox verse.

Free verse allows the poet to admit long polysyllables, and series of polysyllables, that cannot be fitted into meter; it can foster an intense concentration on images and ideas, from which attention will not be distracted by the music of rhyme and meter; it allows great flexibility in the line—tempo can be modulated very subtly, and very powerful emphases are possible; and of course the subtlest and most freely changing rhythms are possible.

Notice the free admission and juxtaposition of polysyllables in these few lines of William Carlos Williams:

> . . . from the deafened
> windows crescendo, rallentando,
> diminuendo.

> ⁓

> . . convoluted, lunging upon
> a pismire, a conflagration.

Rhyme or meter would only blur the clear snapshot of Williams' little imagist picture "The Girl":

> with big breasts
> under a blue sweater

> bareheaded—
> crossing the street

> reading a newspaper
> stops, turns

> and looks down
> as though

> she had seen a dime
> on the pavement.

Williams' poem "The Pink Church" is full of interesting and freely changing rhythms:

> Now,
>   the Pink Church
>   trembles
> to the light (of dawn) again,
>   rigors of more
>   than sh'd wisely
>   be said at one stroke,
> singing!
>   Covertly.
>   Subdued.

Free verse has a number of limitations: (1) Without the guideline of meter, one is sometimes unable to tell exactly how a certain word or syllable is to be stressed. In the following passage there is no metrical principle to help us resolve the ambiguity of emphasis that arises in such words and phrases as *he carries*, *Thus each*, and *that is:*

> With each, dies a piece of the old life, which he carries,
> a precious burden, beyond! Thus each
> is valued by what he carries and that is his soul—
> diminishing the bins by that much
> unless replenished.

(2) Free verse lacks the melodic and mnemonic qualities of rhymed verse. It is such a spare medium that it must compensate by showing extreme deftness of rhythm, or vivid imagery, or expression that is in some other way especially engaging. For example, it seems unlikely that a free verse poem could employ such consistently abstract or generic diction as that of Shakespeare's 129th sonnet or Ben Jonson's poem "To Heaven," and be successful. In those two poems the meter has a strong sensuous impact; it turns the abstractions into pictures and sensations. (3) Since its rule is continual variation, *free verse* cannot gain emphasis for a word by such viable means as inversion of the meter. (4) It invites the prosaic as easily as rhymed verse invites the merely jingling and ornamental. (5) Lacking all formal requirements, it puts the poet wholly on his own. There are no rhymes

to help call up a happy image or idea, no meter to give the poet the feeling that he sees his rhythmic direction and goal clearly.

Traditional prosody results in a "block" typography. We are familiar with that look on the printed page, and we welcome it. The very appearance of a free verse poem can be disheartening. Yet the development of free verse has opened up new possibilities of utilizing space—the blank space of the page—and a few poets today know how to use this space functionally and imaginatively and without affectation or iconoclasm. The freedom in lining, diction, and the deployment of language in general that is inaugurated by free verse has influenced the form of syllabic verse and even of traditional metrical verse. Marianne Moore's syllabic and E. E. Cummings' iambic poems often achieve effects suggested by analogies with free verse poems.

EXAMPLE

A Noiseless, Patient Spider   WALT WHITMAN

A noiseless, patient spider,
I mark'd, where, on a little promontory, it stood, isolated;
Mark'd how, to explore the vacant, vast surrounding,
It launch'd forth filament, filament, filament, out of itself;
Ever unreeling them—ever tirelessly speeding them.

And you, O my soul, where you stand,
Surrounded, surrounded, in measureless oceans of space,
Ceaselessly musing, venturing, throwing,—seeking the spheres. to
    connect them;
Till the bridge you will need, be form'd—till the ductile anchor hold;
Till the gossamer thread you fling, catch somewhere,
    O my Soul.

17
Classical Prosody

Classical Greek and Latin verse is QUANTITATIVE: the metrical structure of the line is based on the *durations* of the individual syllables, rather than on patterns of stresses. Stress was certainly present in Latin and at certain periods was apparently quite prominent; preclassical Latin verse almost certainly employed a stress principle. But in Greek, stress was feeble, although pitch was prominent, as it still is in Chinese. Greek poetry seems to have originated in conjunction with dancing and music; and certainly a need to measure the duration of syllables to fit long and short steps in a dance, or longer and shorter notes in music, must have made a quantitative prosody desirable. The prosodic system survived after Greek poetry had lost its intimate connection with dance and music (just as the practice of writing verse in stanzas continues in English, although poetry is seldom sung today). The Romans aspired to most things Greek, and eventually they adopted the quantitative system for their own poetry. In the early Middle Ages, Latin poetry reverted to stress and adopted rhyme, although rhymeless quantitative poetry continued to be written all through the Middle Ages and the Renaissance.

153

The principles of classical verse are fairly simple. The following paragraphs will serve as an introduction to the fundamental workings of Latin verse of the Golden and Silver periods.

A LONG syllable was, in theory, equal to two SHORT syllables (i.e., the long syllable was thought to take twice the time of utterance of a short syllable): $^-$ = $\smile$ $\smile$.

A syllable is long if it contains (1) a long vowel—these must be learned—as in *māter* or *agrī*; (2) a diphthong, as in *caūsae*, *praēceptum*; (3) a short vowel followed by *x* or *z* or by any two consonants together except an *l* or an *r* (*dūx*, *gāza*, *cāpto*).

A syllable is short if it contains a short vowel followed by another vowel or by a single consonant (*mĕa*, *căvus*).

A COMMON syllable is one whose vowel is short and followed by a mute with *l* or *r*; such syllables may be regarded as either long or short, at the poet's discretion (*săcrificium*, *ăgrī*).

Final syllables that end in a vowel, a diphthong, or *m*, are ELIDED if the next word begins with a vowel or with *h*:

$$- \ \smile \ \smile \ -$$
Odi et amo . . .   *read:* O-det-a-mo.

The most important classical feet are:

iamb	$\smile -$
trochee	$- \smile$
spondee	$- -$
pyrrhic	$\smile \smile$
dactyl	$- \smile \smile$
anapest	$\smile \smile -$
choriamb	$- \smile \smile -$

The most important meter is the DACTYLIC HEXAMETER. This is the meter of the *Iliad*, the *Odyssey*, the *Aeneid*, and the *Metamorphoses*; it was also the basis of much lyric poetry.

Here are lines 5–8 of the *Aeneid*, Book VI:

$$- \ - - \quad - \ - \quad \smile \ \smile \ - \quad \smile \ \smile \quad - \smile\smile \quad - \ -$$
praetex|unt pup|pes. Juven|um manus | emicat | ardens
$$- \smile \ \smile \quad - \smile\smile \ - \quad - \ - \quad - \quad - \smile\smile \quad - \ -$$
litus in | Hesperi|um; quae|rit pars | semina | flammae

‾ ‾ ‾ ‾ ‾ ∪∪ ‾   ‾   ‾∪ ∪ ‾ ∪
abstrus|a in ve|nis silic|is, pars | densa fer|arum

‾∪ ∪ ‾ ‾ ‾ ‾ ‾∪∪ ‾ ∪∪   ‾ ∪
tecta ra|pit sil|vas in|ventaque | flumina | monstrat.

(Impatient, the young men break out of their band and scurry onto
that Hesperus beach: here, some strike up a fire long hidden in the
veins of the flint they find; there, others are scouring the woods full
of discoveries—point out the rivers, and the laired thickets of—
what animals?)

Theoretically, the dactylic hexameter consists of five dactyls and a
spondee as the sixth foot. However, by convention, in any foot
except the fifth a spondee may substitute for a dactyl. Notice, for
example, that the first line of the passage quoted above begins with
two spondaic feet; in the next line the third, fourth, and of course
final feet are spondees. Occasionally a trochee is substituted for the
final spondee, as in the last two lines of the above passage.

    Another very common meter is the H E N D E C A S Y L L A B I C:
an eleven-syllable line of the pattern ‾ ‾ | ‾ ∪ ∪ ‾ | ∪ ‾ | ∪ ‾ ‾. Many
of Martial's epigrams are hendecasyllables:

‾ ‾ ‾ ∪ ∪   ‾∪‾∪ ‾ ∪
Vidi|sti semel, Op|pia|ne, tantum

‾ ‾ ‾ ∪ ∪ ‾ ∪ ‾ ∪‾∪
aegrum | me: male sae|pe te | videbo.

(Oppianus, when I was deathly ill, you came to see me once: I'll see
you ill often.)

By some prosodists the hendecasyllabic line is held to consist of a
spondee (or trochee), a choriamb, two iambs, and a monosyllabic
foot, in that order; others scan it as a spondee, a dactyl, and three
trochees (or two trochees and a spondee). The main pause, or caesura,
is usually after the sixth syllable, sometimes after the fifth.

    The E L E G I A C D I S T I C H (or simply E L E G I A C), another
ubiquitous form, consists of a dactylic hexameter line followed by a
dactylic pentameter; the latter takes the following form:

‾ ‾ ‾ ‾ ‾   ‾ ∪∪ ‾ ∪ ∪‾
procur|rit cas|to || virginis | e gremi|o

or

$$-\cup\cup\;-\quad\cup\cup\quad-\quad-\cup\cup\;-\cup\cup\;-$$
difficile | est. Verum | hoc || qualibet | effici | as.

The scheme is: two and a half feet on each side of a caesura (marked as ||). Spondees are frequently substituted for dactyls in the first half of the line, rarely in the second half.

Martial and Catullus are also fond of the SCAZON, a line of six feet, the first five being iambic, and the final one invariably spondaic:

$$\cup\;-\quad\cup-\cup\;-\quad\cup-\quad\cup-\quad--$$
homo est | venus|tus et | dicax | et ur|banus.

Sometimes the first, and occasionally one other foot is a spondee too:

$$--\;\cup\;-\;\cup\;-\;\cup\;-\quad\cup\;---$$
perscrip|ta, nec | sic ut | fit in | palimp|sesto.

The final spondee slows the line at the end and renders an emphatic effect like the stroke of a hammer. Robert Bridges' poem "Johannes Milton, Senex" is an imitation of the classical scazon; it begins,

$$\cup\;-\cup\;-\cup\;-\;\cup\;-\cup\;---$$
Since I believe in God the Father Almighty.

Schemes of other classical meters—glyconic, alcaic, iambic trimeter, etc.—can be found in the Glossary.

English verse is so powerfully accentual and our ears are so habituated to its accents that quantitative prosody seems quite foreign to us. The English language has many more vowel and consonant sounds than Greek or Latin, hence our quantities never seem fixed as they were in the classical tongues. It is probably impossible to reproduce in English the quality of quantitative lines. The numerous experiments by Campion, Tennyson, Swinburne, Stone, Bridges, and others have produced only a very few poems of any interest at all. It is so unnatural for an English poet to write by quantity, that imagination and spontaneity are likely to be the price of so much artifice. There are, however, a number of sound reasons why an English-speaking poet should study classical prosody and try his hand at imitations: by substituting his native stress principle for the quantitative principle he may find one or more of the classical forms congenial;

and he may be led to pay more attention to the lengths of his syllables, to tempo, and indeed to acoustic quality in general. It would be surprising if an acquaintance with the melodic richness of the vowel and sonorant combinations so ubiquitous and so often assonant in Latin did not suggest new possibilities to an English poet. Such acquaintance was certainly fruitful for Milton and Tennyson; their rich harmonies of vowels are not an especially Anglo-Saxon characteristic. One of Swinburne's best poems is his "Sapphics," and some of Longfellow's best moments are in his "Evangeline," a long narrative poem whose verse line is an imitation of the classical hexameter.

The SAPPHIC stanza has the pattern:

$$— \cup — — — \cup \cup — \cup — —$$
$$— \cup — — — \cup \cup — \cup — —$$
$$— \cup — — — \cup \cup — \cup — —$$
$$— \cup \cup — —.$$

Here are the eighteenth and nineteenth stanzas of Swinburne's "Sapphics":

> All withdrew long since, and the land was barren,
> Full of fruitless women and music only.
> Now perchance, when winds are assuaged at sunset,
>   Lulled at the dewfall,

> By the grey sea-side, unassuaged, unheard of,
> Unbeloved, unseen in the ebb of twilight,
> Ghosts of outcast women return lamenting,
>   Purged not in Lethe.

Notice that Swinburne lets stress fall where it will. Basing his criteria on an analogy with classical prosody, he has decided (with a certain arbitrariness, as we shall see) that certain syllables are short, and certain others long, and he is interested in patterning the quantities only. Thus he considers both syllables of *barren* long, although only the first syllable has a stress; and the same for *fruitless* and *only*. He considers *-ren* in *barren* long because, being at the end of the line, it absorbs the pause; and he considers the first syllable of that word long because in Latin prosody a syllable was usually long if its vowel was followed by two consonants. In English neither *bar-*

nor *-ren* seems to be of any considerable duration. Both syllables of *only* are long because they contain long vowels (though in ordinary English pronunciation, the long *e* sound of *-ly* is slurred). It is doubtful that either syllable of *barren* is actually longer than the supposedly short syllable *was*.

In "Evangeline" Longfellow follows the dactylic hexameter pattern (the verse line of the *Iliad*, the *Odyssey*, and the *Aeneid*):

$$— \cup \cup | — \cup \cup | — \cup \cup | — \cup \cup | — \cup \cup | — —$$

But in many cases his quantities are doubtful. Let us scan the poem's opening two lines as Longfellow himself construed them:

$$— \cup \cup \quad — \cup \quad \cup — \cup \quad \cup \quad — \cup \cup \quad — \quad \cup \quad \cup|$$
This is the | forest pri|meval. The | murmuring | pines and the

$$—\ \ —$$
hemlocks,

$$— \cup \cup \quad — \quad \cup \cup — \ — \quad — \ \cup\cup — \cup$$
Bearded with | moss, and in | garments | green, indis|tinct in

$$\cup \quad — \ —$$
the | twilight . . .

In actuality, the first syllable of *murmuring* can be no longer than the second (it is the very same syllable); and the third syllable *-ing* is, with its resonance, undoubtedly at least as long as *mur-*. Moreover, surely the second syllable of *garments* is longer than the first, even though *gar-* receives the stress. Nevertheless, overall the quantities work out pretty much according to the theoretical pattern, and even when they do not, the verse can be perfectly successful in every respect—rhythm making its ultimate appeal always to the ear rather than to anything else.

18
Prosody and Period

The following is a synopsis, by period, of significant developments in English prosody.

PERIOD	DEVELOPMENTS
Old English (Anglo-Saxon) 449–1066	The ALLITERATIVE LINE (accentual prosody) for all poetry. *Beowulf, Deor, Widsith, The Seafarer, The Battle of Maldon,* runes.
Early Middle English (Anglo-Norman) 1066–1350	Development of ACCENTUAL-SYLLABIC VERSE, the marriage of syllable-counting (the French habit) and stress-counting (the native English habit). Development of IAMBIC AND TROCHAIC METERS, uncertainly and irregularly. Development of RHYME, also uncertainly, as in Layamon's *Brut*. Imitations of Norman rhyming forms. The old alliterative line continues, but is falling into desuetude. Langland's *Piers Plowman* the last important poem to be written in the alliterative meter (c. 1350).

PERIOD	DEVELOPMENTS
Late Middle English 1350–1500	Chaucer (d. 1400): *The Canterbury Tales, Troilus and Criseyde*. This, almost the first regular accentual-syllabic verse, remains among the greatest. Chaucer is also the first Englishman to make the RHYME ROYAL an expressive stanza; in emulation, English poets make it a principal stanza for the next two hundred years.
Early Tudor 1500–1558	The ITALIAN SONNET, OTTAVA RIMA, TERZA RIMA, all introduced by Wyatt (d. 1542). The ENGLISH (SHAKESPEAREAN) SONNET and BLANK VERSE, pioneered by Surrey (d. 1547). Surrey's verse, smoother than Wyatt's, gains the greater favor and sets the fashion.
Elizabethan 1558–1603	Marlowe, Shakespeare, and others develop BLANK VERSE FOR THE THEATRE. The SPENSERIAN STANZA, devised by Spenser for his epic allegory *The Faerie Queene* (Books I–VI complete, 1596). Spenser a great prosodic innovator. Much of his early verse looks backward to Chaucer and to the alliterative tradition. Throughout the Elizabethan age, verse forms of every sort flourish; SONG FORMS and SONNETS especially popular. Prosodic intricacy admired for its own sake: prosody as a form of wit. The Elizabethans were as fond of imaginative and elaborate forms as the Augustans were of the rhymed couplet. Thomas Campion, a musician-poet, disparages rhyme (1602), urges poets to pay more attention to their quantities, and experiments with a kind of quantitative verse. Rebutted by Samuel Daniel in a defense of rhyme (1602).
Jacobean and Caroline 1603–1642	BLANK VERSE continues at a high level in the plays of Ben Jonson, the late plays of Shakespeare, and often in those of John Ford and of Beaumont and Fletcher. The form becomes less regular, and sometimes indistinguishable from prose, in the hands of John Webster, Philip Massinger, and others. John Donne fashions a vigorous, flexible,

PERIOD	DEVELOPMENTS
	conversational idiom that retains an iambic basis and regularity of stanza form. Donne, Jonson, and others bring new prestige to the HEROIC COUPLET inaugurated by Chaucer and illuminated by Christopher Marlowe in *Hero and Leander*. Anglican devotional poetry of greatness by George Herbert (d. 1633), often in intricate and sometimes in emblematic stanza forms; Roman Catholic devotional poetry by Richard Crashaw (d. 1649).
Puritan *1642–1660*	Milton: ITALIAN SONNETS of great power, sometimes ambitiously onomatopoeic; intricate, resonant BLANK VERSE in *Paradise Lost;* unusual metrical freedom and experimentation with rhyme in *Samson Agonistes*. Edmund Waller (d. 1687) and John Denham (d. 1669) favor PENTAMETER COUPLETS and make the form still more popular. Great Anglican devotional poetry in both simple and intricate stanzaic forms by Thomas Traherne (d. 1674) and Henry Vaughan (d. 1695).
Restoration *1660–1700*	HEROIC COUPLETS for all kinds of verse; John Dryden (1631–1700) the master of the form.
Augustan *(Enlightenment,* *Neoclassical)* *1700–1798*	The Age of Reason, of Nature conceived as rational and infinitely manipulable, of Baconian optimism. The great and representative figures: Alexander Pope (1688–1744), Jonathan Swift (1667–1745), Samuel Johnson (1709–1784). Much of the period's first-rate poetry is in COUPLETS, much of that in the CLOSED couplet, which is now held to be the most rational (i.e., most natural) form. Yet the sway of the heroic couplet has been exaggerated. Swift, for example, favored tetrameter couplets through the very heart of the period; and Matthew Prior turned many a fair quatrain. Satiric and didactic verse are the century's main interests; and couplets, of course, are the most pungent of forms. Very few sonnets, none of any value. Prosodic experimentation toward the end of the age

PERIOD	DEVELOPMENTS

(e.g., Gray, Collins). The status of BLANK VERSE in this period is an interesting paradox to which too little attention has been called. Outside the drama, blank verse had practically disappeared for about half a century (1671: Milton, *Paradise Regained*—1730: Thomson, *The Seasons*). It had never been anathematized, however, and generally it retained a theoretical approval even among poets who preferred the couplet for their own verse. To these more "classical" Augustans (e.g., Swift, Pope, Addison), blank verse was acceptable because it was plain and could be brought close to the manner of prose. To the more romantic Augustans (e.g., Thomson, Shenstone, Young) it was attractive for other reasons: it avoided the polished tone and packaging tendency of couplets; its rhymelessness, diminishing aesthetic distance, not only made possible the prosaic quality that was viable for the more rationalistic temperaments, but also could make for an effect of "naturalness" congenial to the "preromantics'" spontaneous enjoyment of meadows, vales, hills, and ruins; also, blank verse connoted Shakespeare and the romantic Elizabethans generally.

Romantic 1798–1832   William Blake (1757–1827), William Wordsworth (1770–1850), and Samuel Taylor Coleridge (1772–1834) are influential in restoring the prestige of a wide variety of forms by restoring the prestige of passion, imagination, exoticism, and strongly asserted individuality. BALLADS regain favor. Wordsworth prizes the ballad stanza for its associations with simple, rustic life; Keats and Coleridge value it more for its associations with an idealized and exotic past. Wordsworth breathes new life into the SONNET. ODE forms are valued, not because of their classical origin, but because they can be employed with a certain looseness and spiritedness, and because they permit patterns of varying line lengths, which in turn can help create an effect of contraction and expansion (rendering unity in variety) once again felt to be admirable in its own right and also felt to resemble the "pulsations" of intense feeling. Blake develops a very free long-lined ACCENTUAL VERSE, and experiments successfully with SLANT RHYME. Blake is a great master of the QUATRAIN. Burns's colloquial SONG FORMS are a splendid achievement. The SPENSERIAN STANZA has exotic and romantic Elizabethan connotations, and attracts Burns, Byron, Shelley, Keats, and others. Keats's *Eve of St. Agnes* is perhaps the finest Romantic poem in this stanza. The later Keats ODES are a great body of controlled lyricism and meditation. Byron revitalizes the OTTAVA RIMA in *Don Juan*. Shelley, in *Ode to the West Wind* and the unfinished *Triumph of Life*, raises the TERZA RIMA to new prestige.

Victorian
1832–1900
Few generalizations about either prosody or taste will stand up. There is an immense variety of verse forms, and much experimentation alongside much conservatism. Imitations of CLASSICAL PROSODY by Tennyson (1809–1892) and Swinburne (1837–1909). WEBSTERIAN BLANK VERSE by Matthew Arnold (1822–1888). Arnold's "'Scholar Gypsy'" stanza an excellence mysteriously unique. FREE VERSE (of inferior quality) by W. E. Henley (1849–1903), and (of greatness) by Walt Whitman (*Leaves of Grass*, 1st ed., 1855). Whitman's free verse was deeply influenced by the King James version of the Bible (a book few of his admirers read or recommend); his line tends to be long, end-stopped, and—in this respect like Spenser's— "beautifully redundant." The RUBAIYAT STANZA by Edward Fitzgerald (1809–1883), a remarkable single achievement. Edgar Allan Poe (1809–1849) experiments in unusual, often highly onomatopoeic, forms. Coventry Patmore (1823–1896) experi-

ments with the COWLEIAN ODE, sometimes achieving greatness in the form. Gerard Manley Hopkins (1844–1889; publ. 1913) develops SPRUNG RHYTHM and a highly alliterative, assonantal, and strongly stressed metric; his sonnets, Italian in form, are the best of the period and among the best of any period. His flashing and dithyrambic idiom exerted an enormous influence on many twentieth-century poets; less well known, but equally remarkable, are several poems that are as quiet and as quietly effective as Patmore's usual vein. Robert Bridges (1844–1930), Hopkins' editor, experiments, not very successfully, with imitations of classical prosody, but develops a relatively successful and historically important SYLLABIC VERSE. One of the most significant prosodic developments of the Victorian age is the perfection of CONVERSATIONAL STYLES within the bounds of regular, fixed metrical form.

Modern
1900–

FREE VERSE by Ezra Pound, Amy Lowell, T. S. Eliot, Basil Bunting, H. D., D. H. Lawrence, William Carlos Williams, Richard Eberhart, and a great many others. Free verse not infrequently showing end rhyme: Louis Zukofsky and Robert Creeley. Pound develops a species of free verse which is often sparer and flatter than Whitman's, and usually shorter lined. W. B. Yeats, a great master of the QUATRAIN, also revives the OTTAVA RIMA, writing several remarkable poems in this unlikely stanza. DRAMATIC BLANK VERSE of a very loose type—sometimes free or accentual verse— by William Butler Yeats and T. S. Eliot. More normal blank verse for the theater by Maxwell Anderson; for lyric and narrative poems by Conrad Aiken, Hart Crane, Robert Frost, Edwin Arlington Robinson, Wallace Stevens. SYLLABIC VERSE made the vehicle of excellent poetry by Elizabeth Daryush, Kenneth Rexroth, Marianne

PERIOD   DEVELOPMENTS

Moore, Dylan Thomas. Elaborate or highly regular verse favored by, for example, E. A. Robinson, Dylan Thomas, J. V. Cunningham, Roy Campbell, Robert Lowell, Richard Wilbur, John Fandel. Freer and more traditional forms seem about equally popular. One of the most striking characteristics of contemporary poetry is its tendency to favor a definite, even rhyming, stanzaic pattern, but to employ a line "played by ear"—a SPEECH-CADENCE LINE, usually with iambic overtones. In rhyme, the preference is for SLANT RHYME, although at the time of this writing ordinary rhyme seems to be gaining the ascendancy again. The undisputed masters of slant rhyme are Yeats, Auden, and Dylan Thomas; the tradition goes back to Emily Dickinson and William Blake. Another salient feature of contemporary poetry is the imaginative and sensitive USE OF SPACE on the printed page.

19
Scansions and Comments

A poem's prosody does not exist apart from its other elements. Indeed, the main point of any analysis of a poem is to observe how every part and aspect of its total structure works in harmony to produce a successful aesthetic experience. Ultimately it is necessary to speak of prosody, imagery, syntax, theme, logical structure, and all other matters in the same breath. The following discussions of specific poems are designed to expose a wide range of prosodic devices and effects functioning as parts of a larger or total system. The first two discussions—on poems by Rossetti and Aphra Behn— will also illustrate various problems in the sheer mechanics of scansion.

I

The Blessed Damozel   DANTE GABRIEL ROSSETTI

The sun | was gone | now; the | curled moon

Was like | a lit|tle feath|er

Fluttering | far down | the gulf; | and now

She spoke | through the | still weath|er.

Her voice | was like | the voice | the stars

Had when | they sang | togeth|er.

lines 55–60

The lament for a dead lady is a well-known poetic type. In "The Blessed Damozel" Rossetti gave the traditional motif a new turn: his poem "determined to reverse the conditions and give utterance to the yearning of the loved one in heaven." It is a highly imaginative piece. The point of view is completely sympathetic. Heaven is treated with the tentativeness and marmoreal quality that seem appropriate; the lady's delicacy, passionate longing, and odd mixture of ethereality and voluptuousness are vividly rendered. The overall effect Rossetti seems to strive for is that of a brilliant and mysterious and tenuous vision about to dissolve. Central to this vision are the beauty of the woman and the beauty of heaven, each made the more intense by an aura of insubstantiality.

Given this intention, Rossetti obviously had no use for certain kinds of rhythms. He did not want great speed, or a gallop, or a robust sprung rhythm, or the staccato of

Oh Galuppi, Baldassaro, this is very sad to find!

In fact, he establishes a rhythm that might be very roughly described as delicate, subtle, hesitant, wavering. How does he achieve these qualities?

Notice the relative absence of strong stress. Several of the words that take the stress (ictus) in their respective feet receive in fact only a light stress: the first *now*, the two appearances of *like*, and *Had*, for example. The result is an absence of stress vigor; or, looked at positively, a certain softness or lightness.

Notice too that the meter itself is rather irregular throughout, and very irregular at certain points. Only two of the six lines conform strictly to the iambic pattern. In the first line, a strong caesura breaks the third foot, and this foot is already inverted into a trochee. The effect is so potent that the sense of iambic pattern becomes very tenuous indeed. The stanza's last line is also odd metrically: *Had* belongs phrasally to the final foot (*the stars*) of the preceding line, and further deviates from the expected pattern in that it commences an inverted foot. Strict metrical regularity usually seems to create an atmosphere of decisiveness or firmness—qualities not wanted here.

The feminine rhymes, too, undoubtedly contribute to the wavering, insubstantial quality of these lines. The absence of stress and the drop in pitch at the ends of the lines create an effect of trailing-off, an effect that is especially acute to an English ear.

Sound color plays its part. The stanza is not by any means mellifluous: *curled*, *gulf*, and *spoke*, for example, have a certain harshness. Yet there is a general euphony, and it is perfectly appropriate. Short vowel and short diphthong sounds are the rule (notice, in this respect, especially line 2). The stanza is far removed from the acoustic heaviness of, say, *Paradise Lost*.

Rossetti was a skillful but conservative metrist. The scansion we have made here is similarly traditional or "classical" and should indicate the pattern in which Rossetti conceived himself to be working. The stanza consists of iambic tetrameters alternating with trimeters that run to an extra syllable at the end. In isolation, the passage might seem to consist of tetrameters alone, every other line being a syllable short (catalectic); but the rest of the poem generally gives us trimeters, never tetrameters; and no portion of a poem must be evaluated apart from its metrical context. A fully responsible reader is no more at liberty to disregard the metrical structure a poet intended than he is to switch the positions of stanzas or to alter the diction of various lines. Or, to put the matter another way, a reader is free to do anything he likes as long as he knows what he is doing.

Most of the variations in the individual feet of these lines are of a traditional type: notice the familiar substitution of trochees, spondees, and pyrrhics for the iambic units. *Fluttering* is a classical instance of elision; by license, it makes a disyllabic foot. Its penultimate syllable is articulated (in British enunciation it is often slurred to the point of being almost inaudible) but is considered too light to be counted in the metrical scheme.

The sense of the passage determines that the following foot (*far down*) will be a spondee. Should *curled moon* be scanned as a spondee too, or as an iamb in which the first syllable is unusually strong? This seems to us a question not leading anywhere: the important point is to see—and no one can avoid seeing it—that the sense of the line demands fair stress on both words.

II

Song   APHRA BEHN

When maid|ens are young, | and in | their spring,

Of pleas|ure, of pleas|ure, let 'em take | their full swing,

Full swing, | full swing,

And love, | and dance, | and play, | and sing,

For Sil|via, believe | it, when youth | is done,

There's nought | but | hum-drum, | hum-drum, | hum-drum,

There's nought | but | hum-drum, | hum-drum, | hum-drum.

—from The Emperor of the Moon

Aphra Behn's vigorous little *carpe diem* song could not be more unlike Rossetti's poem; to take them together is to see at once that the Muse will not be restricted to a single mood or mode. Poetry less indirect, less delicate, and more colloquial hardly exists. And of course the question might even be asked—some fastidious soul will surely ask it—*is* this poetry? The lines are devoid of imagination, in the ordinary sense of the word, although we shall argue for their *prosodic* imaginativeness. The images are conventional and generalized. No fresh metaphor comes into play. There is no economy; in fact, the verse seems to pride itself on its redundancy. And yet the piece is not as ill-made as it might seem; it will grow on one, if given a chance.

A song is meant to be sung. Silent reading, or even reading aloud, will not do. If we remember that, we are well on our way to appreciating Aphra Behn's lyric.

Sung—with or without instrumental accompaniment—what may seem dull or trivial here on the printed page has a chance of becoming exuberant and rhythmically imaginative, incantatory and memorable. If we fail to take the musical context into account—and of course each of us can make up his own tune, it isn't a matter of requiring the original score—the statement seems belabored and the repetitions mere carelessness, bad taste, uninventiveness, or a combination of such defects. In the opening line, *spring* does little more than repeat the idea already established by *young*. In the second, *of pleasure* is repeated. Then follows *full swing*, repeated three times. The closing lines are identical, and *hum-drum* is iterated six times.

Yet the history of the arts shows us that excess is as time-honored a technique as understatement and sparseness. Certainly there is a long tradition of explicitness and of verbal repetition in the song. If we set out to take Aphra Behn's redundancy to task, we may well find that (if we remember to sing) it will have its way with us. The repetitions turn out to be deliberate and artistic. So does the loose metric.

The verbal repetitions help create a general *emphatic* quality, as all controlled repetition tends to do. Singing is a more intense activity than reading. That is, the sheer *fact* of singing reveals an intensified inner energy; something has happened that has resulted in "life enhancement," to use Bernard Berenson's phrase. In the quieter situation of a silent reading, the repetitions seem *too* emphatic, mere delay—but not in singing. One need only sing the piece without its repetitions to hear what a considerably less interesting lyric would result with their absence.

The contrast between the Cyrenaic *full swing* and the monotonous and rhythmically onomatopoeic *hum-drum* is made effective by the repetitions and metrical parallelism (both feet are spondaic). The phrases form a happy antiphony.

The varied feet of the early lines give way in the end to a relentless beat; notice also the disappearance of the rapid, trisyllabic feet.

The whole prosody of the piece is directed toward enacting a spirit of gusto and extemporaneity, and toward dramatizing the contrast between youthful play and adult routine.

The verse is LOGAOEDIC. Notice that the effect of extreme informality is created in part by the very mixture of feet: the pattern is constantly changing its course in a lusty, carefree manner. Iambic-anapestic verse is an ubiquitous English song form (it persists in movie and musical comedy ballads). Notice how important it is to be aware of this tradition: in isolation, the opening lines and the refrain might seem full of amphibrachs:

> When maidens . . .
>
> Of pleasure, | of pleasure,
>
> There's nought but.

A logical scansion can be produced in this way—one that is in fact neater than that adopted here—but such an analysis becomes misleading in that it ignores history.

The third foot of the second line is a "loose anapest," a license occasionally encountered in English verse. The boisterous logaoedics easily accommodate such a moment of metrical recklessness, just as they permit the careless rhyme of *done* with *drum*. The effect of impromptu is essential. In stricter and subtler verse, the license would strike one as mere slovenliness. Notice that the main contribution of all the anapests is speed.

Several other metrical details are interesting. Why, for instance, should *in* (line 1), a relatively unimportant word normally, be marked as a stress? Partly it is sense that dictates the ictus here (what season the maidens are *in* is important), and partly it is the repugnance, to an English ear, of traveling across three distinctly enunciated nonstresses before arriving at a fair beat. This repugnance is unavoidable in the third foot of the second line; but there it is mitigated somewhat since *let* is semantically active enough to call for a secondary stress, and since the first syllable (*-ure*) is not distinctly enunciated. In the context of this general metrical looseness, it is hard to say whether *Sylvia* in the fifth line is meant to be articulated as a dissyllable, which it does become or almost become in British English, or to carry its full three syllables and thus form another loose or four-syllable anapest:

> -vi a be lieve.

The parallel caesuras of the fourth line help isolate each phrase, securing distinct attention for each of the merriments. In fact, every aspect of this line, from grammar to foot structure and degree of stress, stands in parallel, and such marked parallelism is rhetorically emphatic.

The fourth foot of the second line (*their full swing*) illustrates one of the unusual ways in which context may modify stress. In this foot, *full* does not yet possess the same degree of stress as *swing;* it is the repeated pairing of the two words that lends the adjective the full stress it receives in the third line.

III

Epithalamion   EDMUND SPENSER
Wake, now my love, awake; for it is time,
The Rosy Morne long since left Tithones bed,
All ready to her silver coche to clyme,
And Phoebus gins to shew his glorious hed.
Hark how the cheerefull birds do chaunt their laies
And carroll of loves praise.
The merry Larke hir mattins sings aloft,
The thrush replyes, the Mavis descant playes,
The Ouzell shrills, the Ruddock warbles soft,
So goodly all agree with sweet consent,
To this dayes merriment.
Ah my deere love why doe ye sleepe thus long,
When meeter were that ye should now awake,
T'awayt the comming of your joyous make,
And hearken to the birds lovelearned song,
The deawy leaves among.
For they of joy and pleasance to you sing,
That all the woods them answer and theyr eccho ring.

lines 74–91

Spenser wrote the *Epithalamion* for his own marriage in Ireland in 1595; it is one of the world's most splendid occasional poems. Its sustained radiance and buoyancy, its balanced vision of sensuous delight and soaring idealism, have never been matched.

The poem's stanzas consist of either eighteen or nineteen lines rhyming in intricate patterns. Although most of the lines are iambic pentameter, there are also trimeters, and every stanza closes with a hexameter refrain. Such a large stanza is difficult to balance and unify, and perhaps only the inspiration of the occasion carried the poet through. Metrically it is the most elaborate poem of a poet who often favored elaborate forms. The reason seems to be that it is meant as a gift, and a gift for his own bride rather than for someone more remote. The occasion demands something special. But while it is Spenser's most personal poem, it is also suprapersonal: it is a vision of ideal marriage and ideal womanhood, and as such it transcends its occasion. The poem's elaborateness, then, constitutes a paradox: the grandness and the intricacy are an indirection, an oblique declaration, that expresses on the one hand personal involvement of the deepest sort and, on the other, the impersonality of ritual and the transcendent aspect of marriage itself.

The prosody is at once warmth and realized distance. In the vibrancy of this expansive epodic stanza, as in its euphony, we see Spenser's joy in the day and in the prospect of the future. In its largeness and intricacy we see his wish to present a wedding gift suitably generous, hard-wrought, and formal—expensive, as it were. The high elaborateness is, once again, his way of showing his bride how much loving trouble he has gone to, and how delighted he is; at the same time, it is his way of obtaining a formality appropriate to the ritual and to the lofty, sacramental conception of marriage.

Poems of this sort are rare in our day but perhaps not quite extinct. Dylan Thomas's fine lyric "Poem in October," for example, similarly fuses, in its elaborately epodic and cross-rhyming syllabic prosody, ecstasy and the formality and dignity of commemoration.

IV

Song   ALFRED, LORD TENNYSON

Come down, O maid, from yonder mountain height . . .
But follow; let the torrent dance thee down
To find him in the valley; let the wild
Lean-headed eagles yelp alone, and leave
The monstrous ledges there to slope, and spill
Their thousand wreaths of dangling water-smoke,
That like a broken purpose waste in air:

So waste not thou; but come; for all the vales
Await thee; azure pillars of the hearth
Arise to thee; the children call, and I
Thy shepherd pipe, and sweet is every sound,
Sweeter thy voice, but every sound is sweet;
Myriads of rivulets hurrying thro' the lawn,
The moan of doves in immemorial elms,
And murmuring of innumerable bees.

–from *The Princess*, xi, 1, lines 18–31

For a hundred years now the concluding two (and sometimes three) lines of this poem have been justly regarded as not only among the very best in Tennyson but as among the most memorable in English poetry. It is fortunate that they come as the *last* lines of the song: if they appeared in any other position, surely all that followed would be something of an anticlimax. But the fact is that these famous lines, like all others when taken out of context, have only that incomplete kind of beauty and meaningfulness that any fragment may have. In their case, they are by no means merely the redeeming gems of an otherwise indifferent sequence of lines. They exist in a perfectly harmonious relationship with the lines that precede them; they form not only a lovely but also a logical conclusion to all that comes before. The magic of their alliteration and onomatopoeia does not exist for its own sake, but for the sake of the whole song. Similarly, their diction and imagery, while exquisite in themselves, are chosen as much for their logical value in relation to what has come before, as for their independently idyllic qualities. None of the preceding lines is so memorable, yet they are all adroitly fitted to their purposes, and the whole passage is supremely effective.

A shepherd bids his beloved to abandon her mountain home and come down to his love in the valley. He contrasts the cold and harshness of the heights with the fruitfulness of life and love in the valley. The lines are as much a paean to the bucolic joys of the dales as they are anything else. The shepherd traces the course of his beloved's descent: not in an abstract manner but through a succession of images. The detail of this downward journey begins at the line, "But follow; let the torrent dance thee down." Tennyson's dramatic and descriptive techniques bring the reader to an imaginative identification with the girl. The lines convey a sense of rapid downward motion, and of the impatience of the shepherd. They convey also his joyousness, his lyrical feeling for his pastoral home.

The impression of downward movement so strongly, distinctly created in the whole passage is to be accounted for first of all by the progression of the imagery itself. The initial image is of the torrent, which begins in the sky above the mountains themselves; next are described the eagles, which frequent the tops and higher reaches of the mountains, and "yelp alone"; these are followed by pictures of sloping ledges, falling streams, and vales clearly in sight; and finally the girl is among trees and lawns.

Equally important in creating this sense of motion is the fact that the lines are verb centered. The fifteen lines contain no less than fifteen verbs of physical or vocal movement, and three active verbals. This abundance of active and transitive forms charges the passage with movement.

The qualities of the descent are those of speed, breathlessness, and impatience. To gain these effects Tennyson utilizes two devices: (1) enjambment, and (2) division of the lines into short members. Eight of the lines, or more than half, are run-overs; of the remaining six, only two are fully end-stopped. In one place there are four run-on lines in succession, and in another, three. To get even more speed and a sense of the impatience and breathlessness of both lovers, Tennyson breaks most of the lines into short, sometimes choppy, clauses and phrases, averaging only three or four words apiece. The only exceptions to this are the two lines, "Their thousand wreaths of dangling water-smoke / That like a broken purpose waste in air." But even these lines contribute indirectly to the impression of speed. They are intentionally made long and slow by difficult and clustered consonants, resonant sound colors, and syntactical complexity, in order to heighten, by means of contrast, the sense of motion that precedes and leads away from them. That such a contrast is intended is made evident by the ensuing contrast between the streams that "like a broken purpose waste in air" and the admonition, "So waste not thou."

We are now prepared to appreciate the full value of the last three lines. They enact the end of the descent, with the ensuing serenity and the vision of a rich, pastoral life. The motion all but completely disappears, and is replaced by a luxurious restfulness. This effect is created by the sense, but also by stopping the flow of verbs, by allowing the lines to run uninterruptedly, and by employing combinations of vowels and consonants that cannot be uttered swiftly. Even though there is some motion left in the line "Myriads of rivulets hurrying through the lawn," it is lateral, not vertical motion; in any event, it is the *sound* of the rivulets, not their *motion*, to which the poet calls attention. The final two lines become almost entirely placid, with only one gerund (*murmuring*) to indicate motion, and that vocal rather than physical motion.

Note the effective contrast between the imagery of these concluding lines and the imagery that characterizes the barren mountains. Life abounds: lawns, doves, elms, and bees. Light, pleasant rivulets have replaced the dangling, purposeless gushings of the peaks. The strident cry of eagles has given way to the soft moan of doves. The trees are elms not as some too cynical anti-Romantic might suppose because the word *elm* fits the surrounding alliteration of *l*s and *m*s so well, but because much of the English countryside is famous for its abundance of great and ancient elms; the word was a most natural, most correct, choice. The same logic holds for the word *murmuring*. In small numbers, bees merely *buzz;* but semantically speaking the very best English word for describing the sound of *innumerable* bees is *murmuring*. The collocation of *m*s in both lines is fortunate too because it does create a humming tone that brings the reader into the presence of the bees. The abundance of the *l*s is suitable because it creates a sweet, liquid tone complementary to the lyrical and serene feeling of the poem's close.

The passage is, then, a remarkable one. At no sacrifice of logic or clarity, it is magically onomatopoeic in rhythm and in sound color. It vivifies a descent from the mountains by means of images belonging to successively lower and lower altitudes, and by the number of its verbs. It qualifies that movement as swift and impatient, and the lovers' feelings as eager and single-minded, by letting the lines run freely into one another and by breaking them into short breaths. It brings the descent to a conclusion, and the lovers into a lyrical serenity, by ending with long, slow lines and with a final beauty of sound.

V

The Bee   JOHN FANDEL

A zig-zag bee, zzz and zzz-ing came
Out of the flowers in my room; his claim
For being there was he had been carried there
While he worked in a flower, unaware.

He swayed, buzzed toward a window where a screen
Stopped him, sieved the universe between
A green beyond and his desire for
A green beyond: he was neither/nor.

From flowers to screen, he hummed a sort of thunder—
Nothing, yet olympic to my wonder;
His song stopped when the network stopped the bee.
He inspected man's ingenuity.

The screen was there to keep him out, not in.
I wanted to let his ecstasy begin
Again—to let it continue as it was.
Let a bee have his summer: what he does

With his brief season is a song for hours;
Let a bee have his privilege of flowers,
I thought. Therefore, I took an envelope
(He did not know this was his one white hope)

And tried to maneuver him to crawl inside.
Something, maybe fear or maybe pride,
Prompted him to be difficult:
He had his bee-wise reason to consult

Whether this should be or should not be.
I learned some independence from the bee.
Yet, because I could not watch him strive
Futilely, and wanted him alive—

I could not let him die, with honeysuckle
Just in view—I nudged him with my knuckle,
Then carried him outside like a note for mailing.
I opened the envelope, and the bee went sailing

Into his freedom as his thunder began
Again. I felt aliveness as a man
Should. I felt the summer rise in me.
I saw a million flowers for the bee.

In our chapter on rhyme, we discussed a number of uses to which that device may be put. Perhaps an exposition less theoretical will bring out certain points more clearly.

The poem by John Fandel shows a rhyme scheme that is both consistent and ordinary. In fact, the poem is quite "orthodox" in several ways: couplet rhyming, quatrain stanzas, and "full" line length are met with at every turn in English poetry. Even the content of the poem is traditional: there is nothing bizarre, perverse, or esoteric about the experience or about the speaker's attitude toward that experience. It is this pervasive normality that will allow some of our questions and answers about *this* poem to take on a wider applicability.

Why did the poet choose to adopt rhyme for this particular poem? English lyric poetry has been a rhyming poetry for centuries, and so in one sense there is never anything unusual about deciding upon rhyme. And yet perhaps English poetry would have been better off without the device; perhaps we have been in a rut and have lacked the perspective to get out of it.

Is the rhyme suitable to this *particular* poem? How *active* or conspicuous is rhyme in general, and in this poem in particular? What is the effect on the reader or listener?

We shall continue to do more asking than answering. Let us proceed by making some elementary observations.

Rhyme is certainly a *conspicuous* linguistic feature. In some poems it insistently draws our attention—and Fandel's, we think, is such a poem. Under what conditions does rhyme become so magnetic?

Perhaps in verse whose *meter* or line length (or both, as in "The Bee") is quite irregular, the rhyme tends to become conspicuous because it is the one consistent, predictable formal element. Also, conspicuousness will be enhanced in lines that are end paused, since a pause creates emphasis at that point. It is probably true too that *successive* rhyme, as in couplets or triplets, is acoustically more impressive than *alternating* rhyme, especially in complicated alternations in which many of the rhymes are widely separated. The ear and mind seize a short unit readily. Notice that "The Bee" runs along in couplets; and about half the lines are end paused.

To go to even more general considerations: rhyme is relatively conspicuous in any sort of poem, and for reasons not at all arcane. It draws our attention because it is something out of the ordinary; it is a scheme, a ritual, and the reader becomes caught up in it. Our expectation is aroused and then satisfied—or surprised. We find our interest increased, too, in another, related way: we "wonder ahead," curious as to what word will mate with the rhyme word we are now passing beyond. And still another point: coming as it usually does at the end of a line, rhyme falls into a position of rhetorical prominence.

Rhyme is generally, then, a conspicuous element of verse in which it occurs. In "The Bee" it is in fact striking. What if anything justifies the fact that our attention is drawn so insistently to these like endings? Rhyme has at times been condemned as mere "jingle." English poets—a notoriously rhyming species, like the French—have on occasion damned it roundly. Milton and Campion once called it barbarism; William Carlos Williams' attitude may be gathered from the title of his poem, "When Structure Fails Rhyme Attempts to Come to the Rescue." On the other hand, few even of the most ardent "unrhymers" would want to dispose of practically the whole tradition of English lyric verse; few would suggest that Shakespeare or Chaucer would have been better off without it. How seriously dare we take a man who would exclude all rhyme from his theory of the good and the beautiful?

To come back to the poem at hand. It seems to us, and apparently has seemed to a good many people, nearly perfect. One has difficulty not being sympathetic with the speaker's attitude. It is mature and compassionate; the speaker's, and thus indirectly the poet's, sensibility is deep; his ego as we see it here is not notably self-regarding—indeed, the man gives himself over so lovingly to the bee and to the abundance and freedom of summer as to bless these things unconsciously and make the situation and the attendant emotion so vivid as to be physically present for us. Tenderness and strength coexist: note how the verbal economy, the colloquialisms of word and phrase, and the sharp, specific perceptions counteract any tendency toward sentimentality. There is a triumph at the end; the whole poem is pervaded by joy, the kind of joy all of us can still receive even in an age of noise and rush and distracting tensions and massively destructive wars. Joy, beauty, pleasure, playfulness, tenderness, love of order and freedom—one has to draw upon the old traditional words to describe the total attitude expressed in "The Bee."

Does the rhyme seem at odds with such attitudes and qualities? Certainly any sense of play that it creates is perfectly consonant with the speaker's attitude toward his experience; and certainly the order or formality created by the pattern of rhyme is in accord with the speaker's concern for the right order of things, and with the poet's desire to define and vivify an experience he has had or imagined. Making a rhyme scheme is in itself a way of affirming a general commitment to order, of implying both the necessity of order to a high degree of civilization and the immediate aesthetic pleasure inherent in it.

At the same time, the rhyme exists for the sake of the poem, and not vice versa. It adds pleasure and interest to a little narrative that holds one as the situation works itself out, and to an encounter with a rich and controlled sensibility. And by what it says indirectly—a commitment to order and rationality and aesthetic pleasure—it enriches the poem's total meaning.

Glossary

Terms not found here have been defined elsewhere; see Index.

ACATALECTIC

    Literally means, "not defective at the end." Lines that contain the expected number of syllables.

ACCENT

    (1) *Word accent:* The accent which falls on one or more syllables of a word, independently of context; also called *lexical* accent:

    simplý   innocuous   antipathetic.

    (2) *Rhetorical accent:* The accent needed to stress a particular word or meaning in context: "Give *me* the daggers," says Lady Macbeth; normally *Give* would receive more force than *me*.

    (3) *Metrical accent* (also called *ictus*): The accent demanded as a result of the theoretical metrical pattern; word accent and metrical accent nearly always correspond.

ACCENTUAL VERSE

    Verse that constructs its meter by regularizing the number, but not the placement, of accents (stresses) in its lines. Most early Germanic poetry, including Old English, was accentual. The basic scheme of Old English or Anglo-Saxon versification, for example, is as follows: Each line is broken by a strong caesura into two halves (hemistichs);

each half-line contains two strong stresses and an indeterminate number of nonstresses or weaker stresses; two, and often three, of these primary stresses alliterate; most of the whole lines are run-ons (enjambed). Some scholars believe that they discover, in addition, a foot system or a system susceptible to analysis by musical notation; but the conflicting and often complicated theories which have seen such a subtle system within the obvious system suggest that perhaps the metrical scheme is really quite simple after all:

$$
\text{Cóm þa to lánde} \quad \text{lídmanna hélm}
$$
$$
\text{swíðmod swýmman;} \quad \text{saélice gefeáh . . .}
$$

ACOUSTIC METRICS

Theories of prosody based upon rigorous laboratory investigation, including the use of electronic instruments. A brilliant synopsis of the strengths and weaknesses of this school will be found in Wellek and Warren, *Theory of Literature.*

ACROSTIC

A poem in which the initial letters of the successive lines spell a word or words, often a name. Sometimes more intricate patterns of succession are employed (e.g., first letter of the first line, second letter of the second line, etc.). For a witty example of a complex acrostic, see Poe's sonnet "An Enigma."

ADONIC

A classical meter of two feet, sometimes imitated in English. The last line of a SAPPHIC stanza (see Chapter 17) was called an adonic; it consists of a dactyl followed by a spondee:

$$-\cup\cup \quad - -$$
Visere | montes.

$$\sim$$

$$
\text{Túrn to the | wéstward.}
$$

ALCAIC

A rhymeless four-line stanza used by Alcaeus, a Mytilene poet (c. 600 B.C.), and later by Latin poets. Its most common scheme is:

$$
\cup \,|\, - \,\cup\,|\, - \, - \,\|\, - \, \cup \, \cup \,|\, - \, \cup \, \cup
$$
$$
\cup \,|\, - \,\cup\,|\, - \, - \,\|\, - \, \cup \, \cup \,|\, - \, \cup \, \cup
$$
$$
- \,|\, - \, \cup \,|\, - \, - \,|\, - \, \cup \,|\, - \, -
$$
$$
- \, \cup \, \cup \,|\, - \, \cup \, \cup \,|\, - \, \cup \,|\, - \, \cup.
$$

Tennyson's alcaic "Ode to Milton" follows this pattern; it begins:

U – U – – – U U – U U
O mighty mouth'd inventor of harmonies,

U – U – – – U U–U U
O skilled to sing of Time or Eternity,

   – –U – – – U – –
Godgifted organ-voice of England,

  –U U – U U –   U –U
Milton, a name to resound for ages.

ALEXANDRINE

An iambic hexameter; more generally, any line of twelve syllables. The alexandrine is the traditional line of French poetry, and derives its name from often having been employed as the verse line in early popular romances about Alexander the Great.

ALLITERATION

Correspondence in sound between nearby, especially initial, consonants:

It will *f*lame out, like *sh*ining *f*rom *sh*ook *f*oil.

AMPHIBRACH

A classical foot of three syllables, its pattern U – U. It is rare in English.

AMPHIMAC

A classical trisyllabic foot composed of a long syllable on either side of a short. Here are some lines of an English imitation:

  /   .   /
Strive no more.

  /   .   /
Man was made

  / . /
Full of joy,

  / . /
Made to soar.

ANACRUSIS

The result of prefixing with one or two unstressed syllables a line that theoretically should begin with a stressed syllable—

dactylic:

 / . .   / . . / .
Lonely and | lovely as | ocean and . . .

dactylic with anacrusis:

A | wonder that | turned him to | wonder and . . .

An initial *stressed* syllable that does not belong with the initial foot of a line is another form of anacrusis (as in the third line of an ALCAIC stanza; see above).

ANTISTROPHE

The second stanza of a Pindaric ode; also called *counterturn.*

APOCOPATED RHYME

Rhyme in which the terminal syllable of one of the rhyming words is not counted:

joy / buoyant,
trying / lie.

ARSIS

In English and Latin verse, the stressed syllable of a foot; in Greek verse, the unstressed syllable(s).

ASCLEPIAD

(1) *The Lesser Asclepiad*, a classical line of the following meter:

— — | — ∪ ∪ — | — ∪ ∪ — | ∪ ∪ ;

or *The Greater Asclepiad*:

— — | — ∪ ∪ — | — ∪ ∪ — | — ∪ ∪ — | ∪ ∪ .

(2) A classical verse consisting of Greater or Lesser Asclepiads, Glyconics, and Pherecrateans, singly or in combination.

AUBADE

A duet said or sung by lovers at dawn.

BACCHIC, OR BACCHIUS

A trisyllabic foot of the pattern: ∪ — —. The same foot turned about is called an antibacchic.

BAR

A single bar | is used to separate feet, a double bar || to indicate caesura.

BEAT

(1) The metrical stress (*ictus*).
(2) Loosely, rhythm or meter.

– – –
– – –

BOUTS RIMES (*boo remay*)

A game or contest, long popular in France, in which one tries to write a poem on a given set of rhymes or syllables. Or, the resulting verse.

BURDEN

A REFRAIN (*q.v.*).

CADENCE

A useful term describing rhythm that follows the stress and tempo of the spoken language, without being metrical. The poetry, for example, of the King James Bible and of Walt Whitman is cadence poetry.

CAESURA

Any pause, however slight, within a line or at the end of a line. Indicated by the symbol ||. A light caesura is not always signaled by a comma (the use of the comma being optional in many cases, and idiosyncratic with many writers):

In the blest kingdoms meek || of joy and love,

ᢙᢒ

Purge and disperse, || that I may see and tell.

If a caesura occurs at the end of a line, the line is said to be *end-stopped;* a line that terminates without a pause and runs directly into the succeeding line is *enjambed.* The most common positions for caesuras are at the end of the line and somewhere toward the middle:

Grace was in all her steps, || Heav'n in her Eye, ||
In every gesture || dignity and love.

Caesuras are least common after the first syllable of a line, and before the last; because of the unusualness of these positions, a caesura there surprises one into attention and may cause the opening or closing word of a line (if it is a stressed monosyllable) to be very emphatic; one of the most striking instances occurs in *Paradise Lost,* Book III, line 42 (quoted below). Relative absence of caesuras—especially of heavier caesuras—in a sequence of lines contributes to the production of a flowing quality; such a passage is likely to be rather involved grammatically and conceptually. Long lines—pentameters, hexameters, septameters—invite caesuras (both terminal and internal) because they tax the breath. The English hexameter (the alexandrine) has a notorious disposition to break with a medial caesura:

And with thy punishment || his penance shalt supply.

Eighteenth-century poets, who looked so favorably on balance and antithesis, often employed medial caesura in their heroic couplets in order to obtain still another effect of symmetry:

As hags hold sabbaths, || less for joy than spite, ||
So these their merry || miserable night.

Seeing to it that the weights and positions of caesuras vary in a sequence of lines is one way by which verse creates rhythmical interest and avoids monotony. Notice that in the following passage from *Paradise Lost* (III, lines 38–48) no two successive lines show caesuras at identical positions:

as the wakeful Bird
Sings darkling, || and in shadiest Covert hid
Tunes her nocturnal Note. || Thus with the Year
Seasons return, || but not to me returns
Day, || or the sweet approach of Ev'n or Morn, ||
Or sight of vernal bloom, || or Summer's Rose, ||
Or flocks, || or herds, || or human face divine; ||
But cloud instead, || and ever-during dark
Surrounds me, || from the cheerful ways of men
Cut off, || and for the Book of knowledge fair
Presented with a Universal blanc. ||

Caesuras are wholly independent of meter: they are determined solely by syntax; that is, by the natural phrasing of the language.

CANTO

A major division of a long poem; for example, Ezra Pound's *Cantos*, and the cantos of Dante's *Divine Comedy* and of Spenser's *Faerie Queene*.

CANZONE

A Renaissance Provençal and Italian stanza of varying length and rhyme scheme, a common vehicle for lyrical and meditative poetry. Continental canzones often ran to ten, twelve, or more lines; they influenced a number of Elizabethan poets, for example, Spenser.

CATALECTIC

A line that has, at its end, a syllable less than the line requires. The first line below is acatalectic (has the regular number of syllables), the second catalectic:

Forced to | the pris|on, from | the pris|on haled.

᰷

Life is | but an | empty | dream. |

CHANT ROYAL

A French stanza form, and a variant of the *ballade*, containing five ten-line or eleven-line ballade stanzas together with a four-line (sometimes a five-line) envoi, each stanza employing the same rhyme sounds. According to one pattern, the stanza rhymes *ababccddedE*, the envoi *ddedE*, the capital letter designating the refrain.

CHOLIAMBIC

The scazon (see Chapter 17).

CHOREUS

In classical verse, a synonym for the trochee (trochaeus).

CHORIAMB

A classical foot composed of a long, two shorts, and a long, in that order: $- \cup \cup -$.

COLOR

A term widely used in acoustics, phonetics, and prosody (and adopted in this book) to designate the quality of sound determined by the material make-up and design of a vibrating part or instrument. (Color is also influenced by the medium through which the sound travels.) In addition, some writers, pressing an analogy between phonological quality and visual quality, speak of "bright" and "dark" colors.

COMMON METER

The ballad stanza.

CRETIC

The AMPHIMAC (*q.v.*).

DIAERESIS

Correspondence of the beginning and ending of feet with the beginning and ending of words:

More than | enough | am I | that vex | thee still.

Long-sustained diaeresis is monotonous.

DIBRACH

A synonym (rarely used) for a pyrrhic foot: ∪ ∪ or ˙˙.

DIMETER

Meter of two feet to a line:

Thy summer's play
My thoughtless hand
Has brushed away.

DISPONDAIC

In classical verse, a foot of four long syllables.

DISTRIBUTED STRESS

See HOVERING ACCENT.

DITHYRAMB

A term used to describe poetry of an exceptionally shrill or ecstatic (and often irregular) nature. Originally it was a passionate song or chant in the rites of Dionysus. Dithyrambic is an apt epithet for much of the poetry of Walt Whitman or Robinson Jeffers.

DOGGEREL

Crude, usually loose or irregular, verse. Rhyme without reason, it might be called. Walter Bagehot's definition is a good one: "People expect a 'marked rhythm' to imply something worth marking; if it fails to do so they are disappointed. They are displeased at the visible waste of a powerful instrument; they call it 'doggerel,' . . . the burst of metre . . . incident to high imagination, should not be wasted on petty matters which prose does as well. . . ."

ELISION

Indicated by the symbols ‿ or '. Elision is the omission of a syllable, or the slurring together of two syllables (or the fiction of doing so), as a way of allowing the meter and syllable count of a line to remain intact:

Th' expense of spirit in a waste of shame;

Yet dearly‿I love you and would be loved fain.

EMBLEMATIC PROSODY

A more inclusive term might be "visual prosody." A poem or part of a poem may be so arranged on the printed page as to become a visual representation of its subject or of its basic metaphor. A poem seeks to gain absolute attention for the quality of human experience it deals with. All of its features—semantic, grammatical, rhetorical, prosodic—contribute to this end; even typographical picturing may be useful. The lines of George Herbert's poem "The Altar" are alternately lengthened and shortened to form a typographical altar. The opening section of Henry Vaughan's "The Waterfall" pictures by line arrangement the water above the falls, the water going down, and the stream below rising again. In William Carlos Williams' *Paterson*, a conflagration is represented by scrambled typography. Ezra Pound, in one of the *Cantos*, makes physical position emphatic:

Here are lynxes   Here are lynxes

ENJAMBMENT

The running of one line into another, without pause or with very light pause unsignaled by punctuation:

Happy those early days when I
Shined in my Angell-infancy!

See also CAESURA.

ENVOI, ENVOY

Literally, a "sending on its way." In prosody, it is a short stanza, usually of four or five lines, concluding a ballade or other French form.

EPITRITE

A classical foot of four syllables, three long and one short, in any combination:

$$- \cup - - \qquad - - - \cup$$
canna cornu   causae clades

EPODE

The third stanza of a Pindaric ode; also called *stand*.

EPODIC

Alternating longer and shorter lines, as in most English odes, and in much other verse.

EQUIVALENCE

In classical verse, the notion that since all syllables had a fixed quantity (all syllables were equally short or long) one foot might be substituted for another so long as the time intervals remained the same (e.g., a spondee might substitute for a dactyl).

EXTRAMETRICAL SYLLABLE

> An extra syllable, usually light, occurring within the line, not at the end, and not interpreted as really breaking the metrical pattern:

> With thy exuberant flesh so fair.

> The line above remains iambic tetrameter despite the fact that *exuberant* is four, not three, syllables.

FOOT

> A syllable, or a group of syllables, constituting a metrical unit in verse. First used in reference to English poetry by George Gascoigne (1572).

FOURTEENER

> An iambic septameter (fourteen syllables) popular in England in the late sixteenth and early seventeenth centuries, but rarely used thereafter. Chapman's *Iliad* is in this measure:

> All full of turnings, that was like the admirable maze
> For fair-haired Ariadne made by cunning Daedalus.

GLYCONIC

> A classical meter consisting of a spondee, a choriamb, and an iamb, in that order:

> $$- \quad - \quad - \cup\cup- \quad \cup-$$
> *Non   hoc | pollicitus | tuae.*

HEMISTICH(S)

> Half of a line, when the line is well broken by a caesura. Also verse such as Old English written in halved lines:

> Lo! We have heard ‖ how in days of yore
> The Spear-Danes ‖ did deeds of valor.

HENDECASYLLABIC,
HENDECASYLLABLE

> An eleven-syllable line; the traditional line of Italian poetry, and a common form of Latin verse. Rare in English.

HEURISTIC

> In prosody, the stimulating, suggestive, and beneficently limiting qualities that the poet finds in the form he has chosen

HEXAMETER

> Meter of six feet. Often, a synonym for the ALEXANDRINE.

HEXASTICH

A stanza of six lines.

HIATUS

A pause necessitated by the abutting of two identical or similar sounds:

lo*ve v*olume   n*o o*pen

HOKKU

The haiku (see Chapter 17).

HOVERING ACCENT,
DISTRIBUTED STRESS

Usually indicated by the symbol ⌢. A peculiar effect that comes about as a result of conflict between the natural (lexical) stress of a word and the expected or theoretical stress pattern of the verse:

And Í | have leáve | to gó, | of hér | goo͡dness—

Theoretical pattern:

· / · / · / · / · /

Actual pattern:

· / · / · / · / / /

Hovering accent is thus a kind of "blurred" stress. It may come about whenever there is uncertainty about the degree of stress that should be given to two consecutive syllables, both of which are relatively prominent according to sense:

The dáy | want sún, | and sún | want bríght,

The níght | want sháde, | the dea͡d | men gráves.

HUM(S)

The nasals (*n, m, ng*). A category of sound color.

HYPERCATALECTIC

A line that has an extra syllable at the end is called hypercatalectic.

IAMBIC TRIMETER

A classical meter consisting of six iambic feet (the quantitative equivalent of a modern iambic hexameter or Alexandrine):

U – U – U – U – U – U –
gemelle Castor et gemelle Castoris.

ICTUS

The metrical stress. See ACCENT.

IDYLL

A pastoral poem.

INVERSION

The substitution of one metrical foot for another that is identical with it but turned about (as a trochee for an iamb, a dactyl for an anapest).

IONIC

A Greek meter of two feet existing in two forms: Ionic *a majore* and Ionic *a minore*. The former consists of a spondee followed by a pyrrhus; the latter is the same foot inverted:

/ / . .   . . / /
Suns rage and the   And the suns rage.

JUNCTURE

A term, employed by linguists and by some prosodists, roughly equivalent to CAESURA.

KYMOGRAPH

A laboratory instrument by which certain acoustic qualities were formerly measured. Now obsolete.

LEONINE RHYME

Internal rhyme in which one of the rhyming words is at the end of the line and the other immediately preceding the main caesura:

For the moon never *beams* ‖ without bringing me *dreams*.

LICENSE

Metrical variation held by poets to be permissible within a certain kind of verse; as the substitution of spondees for dactyls in the classical hexameter, or trochees for iambs in English iambic verse. Sometimes refers to syntactical liberty.

LINK RHYME

A rhyming sound that results when the last syllable of one line joins with the first sound or syllable of the next:

Phoebus in his bright *car*
Drives Diana all *unstarred*.

LOGAOEDIC

Literally, "prose song." A term, used by English as well as by Greek and Roman writers, to describe verse of mixed meters, as lines of iambic and anapestic, or of trochaic and dactylic, feet. The meter supposedly suggests informality or even prose rhythms:

I kicked | the cat | and I kicked | the door,

I'm sure | the inn|keeper thought | me a boor.

MACRON

The mark ‾, denoting a long syllable. Used by some English metrists to indicate stress.

MADRIGAL

An Italian song form very popular in Elizabethan England. Petrarch's madrigals are usually eight, nine, or ten lines, with all sorts of rhyme schemes. English madrigals vary so greatly in length and in rhyme scheme that no formal definition is possible. They are sung contrapuntally.

My love in her attire doth show her wit,
    It doth so well become her;
For every season she hath dressings fit,
    For winter, spring, and summer,
    No beauty she doth miss
    When all her robes are on;
    But beauty's self she is
    When all her robes are gone.

METER

The determinate acoustic structure of the line:
(1) *Quantitative:* regular alternation of "long" and "short" syllables:

dactylic hexameter

$-\;\cup\cup\;-\quad--\;\cup\cup-\cup\cup\;-\cup\;\cup\;-\;\cup$
Rusticus | ex Mal|o sapi|dissima | poma quo|tannis . . .

(2) *Syllabic:* fixed number of syllables in the line:

decasyllabic

She comes over the lawn, the young heiress,
from her early walk in her garden-wood . . .

(3) *Accentual:* fixed number of stresses in the line:

accentual pentameter

And the wíld hórses frésh in the frésh gráss,
Hórses for mén who ríde as the góds ríde . . .

(4) *Accentual-Syllabic:* fixed number and positions of syllables and stresses in the line:

iambic pentameter

Práy thee | take cáre, | that tak'st | my boóke | in hánd,
To reáde | it wéll: | that ís, | to un|derstánd.

(5) *Some Metrical Units (Feet)*

Iambic	·/ or ∪—
Trochaic	/· or —∪
Pyrrhic	·· or ∪∪
Spondaic	// or ——
Anapestic	··/ or ∪∪—
Dactylic	/·· or —∪∪
Amphibrachic	·/· or ∪—∪
Amphimacic	/·/ or —∪—

MOLOSSUS

A classical foot of three long syllables: — — —

MORA

The mark ∪, denoting a short syllable. Used by some English metrists to denote an unstressed syllable.

MORPHEME

The smallest meaningful or "designative" unit of language. In the word *unwanted*, *un-* is a morpheme because it designates a negative. The *un-* in *uncle*, however, is nonsignificant and therefore not a morpheme.

MUSICAL THEORY

A metrical theory and system of scansion based on the notion that verse rhythm is like musical rhythm and may best be represented by musical notation. The classic exposition is William Thomson's *The Rhythm of Speech* (1923). Other notable adherents are Joshua Steele (1779), Sidney Lanier (1880), George R. Stewart, Jr. (1922), M. W.

Croll (1923), Katherine Wilson (1929), Thomas Taig (1929), and John C. Pope (1942). According to this theory, rhythm comes about when a series of sounds displays exact time relations. In Lanier's conception, verse rhythm "is precisely the same as rhythm in music, the sole difference being that one is suggested to the ear by speech-sounds, the other by music-sounds." The bar is measured from stress to stress. The theory's most vigorous opponents are those who are strongly attracted to acoustic metrics (e.g., Schramm, Sonnenschein). The musical theory is "orthodox" in that it identifies rhythm with regularity. In the view of the present writers such an identification is fallacious, and the temporal regularity of English meters has not been demonstrated (and is unlikely).

OCTOMETER

Meter of eight feet to a line. Rare.

OCTOSYLLABIC

Lines of eight syllables. The octosyllabic couplet is an ubiquitous English verse form. It is usually iambic and often shows a great deal of truncation.

OLD ENGLISH VERSIFICATION

See ACCENTUAL VERSE.

PAEON

A classical foot composed of four syllables, three short and one long, in any combination.

PANTOUM, PANTUN

A Malayan stanzaic form, rarely imitated in English, consisting of quatrains that rhyme *abab*, *bcbc*, *cdcd*, etc., and ending with the *a*-rhyme.

PETRARCHAN SONNET

(1) A sonnet that follows the conventional situations and attitudes of Courtly Love.

(2) A sonnet in the Italian form, with octave and sestet.

PHALAECEAN

A synonym for the classical HENDECASYLLABLE (*q.v.*).

PHERECRATEAN

A classical tripodic meter consisting of an iamb or trochee, a dactyl, and a trochee or spondee, in that order:

∪ – – ∪ ∪ – ∪
Puell|aeque ca|namus.

PHONE

The smallest distinguishable speech sound: thus the *k* consonant phoneme consists of a number of phones (e.g., the voiceless *k* of *broke* and the voiced *k* of *kin*). A SYLLABLE (*q.v.*) is best defined in terms of phones.

PHONEME

The smallest unit of speech that can serve to distinguish one utterance from another: thus, *silk* and *milk* each contain four phonemes, only the initial one being different:

s i l k   m i l k.
1 2 3 4   1 2 3 4

PHONETICS

The science of speech sounds.

POULTER'S MEASURE

A rhymed couplet, the first line iambic hexameter, the second septameter, and both lines perfectly regular (no inversions, substitutions, or unusual caesuras). It was popular in the Early Tudor period:

And in my wife I find such discord and debate,
As no man living can endure the torments of my state.

PROCELEUSMATICUS

In classical verse, a foot of four short syllables: $\cup\cup\cup\cup$.

PYTHIAMBIC

A classical meter consisting of couplets of dactylic hexameter and iambic trimeter. The oracles of Delphi were said to have been delivered in this meter:

$- \cup\cup \quad - \quad - \quad - \quad \cup\cup - \quad - \quad - \cup\cup \ -\cup$
Aemula | nec vir|tus Capu|lae nec | Spartacus | acer

$\cup - \quad \cup - \cup \ - \cup-\cup \ -\cup -$
Novis|que re|bus in| fide|lis All|obrox.

QUATORZAIN

A fourteen-line stanza other than a sonnet.

QUINTET

A five-line stanza (also called a cinquain).

REFRAIN

(1) *Normal refrain:* Verbatim repetition of a line, usually at the end of successive stanzas. A way of helping to organize a poem, of

emphasizing the main theme, of reintroducing a certain tone, and of allowing the participation of a group of singers in a basically solo performance.

There is a garden in her face
Where roses and white lillies grow;
  A heav'nly paradise is that place,
Wherein all pleasant fruits do flow.
  There cherries grow which none may buy
  Till cherry-ripe themselves do cry.

Those cherries fairly do enclose
Of orient pearl a double row,
  Which when her lovely laughter shows,
They look like rosebuds filled with snow.
  Yet them nor peer nor prince can buy,
  Till cherry-ripe themselves do cry.

Her eyes like angels watch them still;
Her brows like bended bows do stand,
  Threat'ning with piercing frowns to kill
All that attempt with eye or hand
  Those sacred cherries to come nigh,
  Till cherry-ripe themselves do cry.

(2) *Incremental refrain:* A refrain that changes its form somewhat from appearance to appearance. See Sir Walter Ralegh's "The Lie" or Spenser's "Epithalamion."
  Refrains are notoriously more effective when a poem is read aloud or sung. When skillfully handled, they not only realize the power potentially wielded by any form of repetition, they can become a distillation of the poem's central tone and vision, haunting the memory. Like other prosodic features, they also help to elicit a profound attention: they create and then fulfill expectation as the poem progresses. A musical analogy is the *rondo*, a form in which a melody or motif is returned to again and again in the same notation. Refrains are truly oral and musical devices; silent reading, because it is an "impatient" situation, robs them of their vitality.

REPETEND
  A refrain or other repeated measure or locution.

RESONANCE

    (1) SONORITY (*q.v.*).

    (2) A category of sound color; characterized by a prolongation and fullness of sound, as frequently with *n, m, ng, z, zh*.

RHYME SCHEMES (a partial list)

Couplet	*aa*
Triplet	*aaa*
Ballad Stanza	*xaxa* or *abab*
Rubaiyat Stanza	*aaxa*
In Memoriam Stanza	*abba*
Limerick	*aabba*
Stave of Six	*ababcc*
Rhyme Royal	*abábbcc*
Triolet	*abaaabab*
Ottava Rima	*abab_abcc*
Common Octave	*ababcdcd* or *xaxaxbxb*
Brace Octave	*abbaabba* or *abbacddc*
Spenserian Stanza	*ababbcbcc*
Ballade	*ababbcbc*

RIME RICHE, RICH RHYME

    Rhyme of the same words (*rich–rich*) or of homonyms (*loan–lone*).

RIME SUFFISANTE

    Ordinary rhyme.

SCANSION

    Analysis of verse to determine the metrical structure.

SEPTENARY

    A line of seven feet or seven stresses. Commonly a synonym for ballad meter in which the tetrameter and trimeter lines are written together as one long line:

    As I in hoary winter's night stood shivering in the snow.

SEPTET

    A seven-line stanza.

SHORT COUPLET

    A tetrameter couplet

SHORT MEASURE

    An iambic trimeter quatrain in which the third line is tetrameter; the rhyme scheme is either *abcb* or *abab*.

SKELTONICS

Certain verses of John Skelton (c. 1460–1529) or verse in their manner. Successions of short, deliberately irregular, loosely accentual lines of two (sometimes three) stresses, often rhyming on the same sound for three, four, five, or more lines:

But to make up my tale,
She breweth noppy ale,
And maketh thereof port sale
To travellars, to tynkers,
To sweters, to swynkers,
And all good ale drynkers,
That wyll nothynge spare,
But drynke tyll they stare
And brynge themselfe bare,
With, Now away the mare,
And let us sley care,
As wyse as an hare!

SLACK

The unstressed syllable or syllables of a foot: in a dactyl, for example, the two syllables following the stress are the slack.

SONOGRAPH

A sound spectrograph; an acoustics laboratory instrument.

SONORANT

A voiced sound of soft quality but rather full volume, including the semivowels *w* and *y*, and the consonants *m*, *n*, *l*, *r*.

SONORITY

Deep, resonant sound. The most sonorous sounds are the vowels.

SPRUNG RHYTHM

A prosody named and discussed by G. M. Hopkins, and employed in a number of his poems. Sprung rhythm is like free verse in that there is no regular succession of feet. The stress pattern varies continually. Alliteration and frequent juxtapositions of strong stresses identify the form; end rhyme, often of a bold or imaginative kind, is also employed.

As a dare-gale skylark scanted in a dull cage
    Man's mounting spirit in his bone-house, mean house, dwells—
    That bird beyond the remembering his free fells;
This in drudgery, day-labouring-out life's age.

STRESS SHIFT

> INVERSION (*q.v.*).

STROPHE

> (1) A stanza or division.
>
> (2) The first stanza of a Pindaric ode, also called the *turn*.

SYLLABLE

> A unit of speech sound which may be uttered with a single expulsion of breath. It consists of one or more PHONES (*q.v.*), one of which has relatively great sonority. Thus, in the syllable *it*, the vowel is sonorous, the consonant not. In the syllable *il*, the consonant is more sonorous than the *t*-sound of *it*, but still less sonorous than the vowel.

SYNALEPHA

> The omission of the first vowel sound in two adjacent vowels; or, their fusion into a single sound, as in
>
> The sun is down and *th' e*vening's nightingales . . .
>
> Also called variously syneresis, synizesis, and elision. Some writers try to maintain technical distinctions among these terms.

SYNCOPATION

> The simultaneous presence of two different patterns of accentuation in a line of verse, as, for instance, when the metrical pattern is counterpointed by the speech rhythm—
>
> *Metrical pattern:*
>
> Let me | not wan|der in | a bar|ren dream;
>
> *Speech rhythm:*
>
> Let me | not wander | in a barren dream.

TAIL-RHYME STANZAS

> Various kinds of stanzas of alternating shorter and longer lines; the shorter lines rhyme with one another and follow intervals of longer lines:
>
> Still thou art blest compar'd wi' me!
> The present only toucheth thee:
> But oh! I backward cast my e'e
>   On prospects drear!
> An' forward tho' I canna see,
>   I guess an' fear!

TELESTICH

An acrostic in which the terminal letters of the lines form a word or words.

TETRAMETER

Meter of four feet or stresses to a line.

THESIS

In English and Latin verse, the unstressed syllable of a foot; in Greek verse, the stressed syllable.

TIMBRE

A synonym for sound color.

TRIBRACH

$$\cup\cup\ \cup$$

A classical foot of three short syllables: *et aqua.*

TRIMETER

Verse of three feet or stresses to a line.

TRIPODIC

A verse line of three feet or parts:

My girl, | thou gaz|est much
Upon | the gold|en skies.

TRUNCATION

Indicated by the symbol $\wedge$. The cutting off of the first syllable of a line, or the omission of an expected syllable within the line:

$\wedge$ I have seen them $\wedge$ gentle, tame, and meek.

The insertion of a syllable at either point would convert this line into iambic pentameter—which, in context, is what one expects it to be.

VERSET

Originally a French term, but adopted by English writers, for the kind of prose that most closely resembles verse (e.g., some of the Tyndale and Authorized Version Psalms; parts of Macpherson's Ossian). In a verset every other stressed syllable is a strong, usually a primary, stress:

He shall feed me in a green pasture, and lead me forth beside the

waters of comfort.

VERSIFICATION

Synonym for prosody. Metric(s), rhythmics, scansion, and other terms are also in use.

VIRELAY

A very elaborate French verse form running on two rhymes or on link rhyme; almost unused in English.

WHEEL

A one-line refrain of rhythm, rather than of words, coming at the end of a stanza. The meter of the wheel line is markedly different from that of the stanza to which it is attached. The wheel stanza is almost unknown outside Middle English poetry.

WRENCHED ACCENT

Domination of word accent by metrical accent; found frequently in folk and literary ballads, in the poetry of Wyatt, and in modern advertising. It is a common occurrence in songs, where the musical accent may not coincide with ordinary speech accentuation—

Speech accentuation:

Kiss Jenny to be sure;

Metrical or musical wrenching:

Kiss Jenny to be sure.

A Selected Bibliography

Works followed by an asterisk are so widely available that no bibliographical
information has been supplied.

B.C.

c. 350   Aristotle. *Poetics*. Text, trans., and commentary in S. H. Butcher,
Aristotle's Theory of Poetry and Fine Art, 4th ed. New York:
Dover Publications, 1951.

A.D.

96   Quintillian. *Oratory (Institutio Oratoria)*, ed. H. E. Butler.
4 vols., Loeb Classical Library, London, 1920–22.

c. 100   Longinus. *On the Sublime*, trans. W. Rhys Roberts, 2d ed.
London: Cambridge University Press, 1907.

1560   Thomas Wilson. *The Arte of Rhetorique*, ed. G. H. Mair.
London: Oxford University Press, 1909.

1575   George Gascoigne. *Certayne Notes of Instruction*, in *Elizabethan
Critical Essays*, ed. George Gregory Smith. 2 vols.; London:
Oxford University Press, 1904.

1586   William Webbe. *A Discourse of English Poetrie*, in *Elizabethan
Critical Essays*, ed. George Gregory Smith. 2 vols.; London:
Oxford University Press, 1904.

1589   George Puttenham. *The Arte of English Poesie*, ed. Gladys
Willcock and Alice Walker. London: Cambridge University
Press, 1936.

203

1595 Sir Philip Sidney. *An Apologie for Poetrie*, in *Elizabethan Critical Essays*, ed. George Gregory Smith. 2 vols.; London: Oxford University Press, 1904.

1602 Thomas Campion. *Observations on the Art of English Poesie*, in *Campion's Works*, ed. Percival Vivian. London: Oxford University Press, 1909.

1603 Samuel Daniel. *A Defence of Ryme*, in *Elizabethan Critical Essays*, ed. George Gregory Smith. 2 vols.; London: Oxford University Press, 1904.

1668 John Dryden. *An Essay of Dramatic Poesy.**

1700 John Dryden. "Preface" to *The Fables.**

1702 Edward Bysshe. *The Art of Poetry*. London.

1755 Samuel Johnson. "Prosody" in *The Dictionary.**

1756 Edmund Burke. *The Sublime and Beautiful* (*A Philosophical Enquiry into the Origin of Our Ideas of the Sublime and Beautiful*). London: Routledge and Kegan Paul, 1958.

1777 David Hume. "Of Tragedy," in *Essays, literary, moral, and political*. London: Ward, Lock.

1779 Joshua Steele. *Prosodia Rationalis*.

1779–1781 Samuel Johnson. *Lives of the Poets.**

1783 J. Beattie. *Theory of Language*.

1786 Thomas Jefferson. "Thoughts on English Prosody." Available in George Hemphill, ed. *Discussions of Poetry: Rhythm and Sound*. Boston: D. C. Heath & Company, 1961.

1800 William Wordsworth. "Preface" to *Lyrical Ballads.**

1804 William Mitford. *Inquiry into the Harmony of Languages*.

1817 Samuel Taylor Coleridge. *Biographia Literaria.**

1838 E. Guest. *A History of English Rhythms*. London: Wm. Pickering.

1878 Coventry Patmore. *Amelia*. London: G. Bell & Sons. [Contains the "Essay on English Metrical Law."]

1880 Edmund Gurney. *The Power of Sound*. London: Smith, Elder.

1880 Sidney Lanier. *The Science of English Verse*. New York: Charles Scribner's Sons. Reprinted in *Works*. Centennial ed.; Baltimore: Johns Hopkins Press, 1945.

1886 Joseph B. Mayor. *Chapters on English Metre*. London: C. J. Clay and Sons. 2d ed., rev. and enl., 1901.

1886 George Lansing Raymond. *Poetry as a Representative Art*. New York: G. P. Putnam's Sons.

1888   Henry Sweet. *A History of English Sounds*. Oxford: Clarendon Press.

1891   Rev. James C. Parsons. *English Versification*. Boston: Sibley and Company.

1891   Felix Schelling. *Poetic and Verse Criticism of the Reign of Elizabeth*. Philadelphia: University of Pennsylvania Press.

1892   Hiram Corson. *A Primer of English Verse*. Boston: Ginn and Company.

1893   John Laurence. *Chapters on Alliterative Verse*. London: H. Froude.

1895   John Addington Symonds. *Blank Verse*. New York: Charles Scribner's Sons.

1898   Alice Edwards Pratt. *The Use of Color in the Verse of the English Romantic Poets*. Chicago: University of Chicago Press.

1899   William Johnson Stone. *On the Use of Classical Metres in English*. London: H. Froude.

1901   Julia Parker Dabney. *The Musical Basis of Verse*. New York: Longmans, Green & Co.

1901   B. Ten Brink. *The Language and Metre of Chaucer*. Trans. M. B. Smith. London: Macmillan & Co.

1903   Joseph B. Mayor. *A Handbook of Modern English Metre*. London: Cambridge University Press.

1903   T. S. Omond. *A Study of Metre*. London: G. Richards.

1906–1910   George Saintsbury. *A History of English Prosody*. 3 vols.; London: Macmillan & Co.

1908   Robert Frederick Brewer. *Orthometry: The Art of Versification*. Edinburgh: John Grant.

1909   Charles F. Richardson. *A Study of English Rime*. Hanover, N.H.

1910   J. W. Bright and R. D. Miller. *The Elements of English Versification*. Boston: Ginn and Company.

1910   Albert H. Licklider. *Chapters on the Metric of the Chaucerian Tradition*. Baltimore: J. H. Furst.

1910   Jacob Schipper. *A History of English Versification*. Oxford: Clarendon Press.

1911   Brander Matthews. *A Study of Versification*. Boston: Houghton Mifflin Company.

1912   Gilbert Murray. "What English Poetry May Still Learn from Greek," *Essays and Studies by the English Association*, 3, 7–31.

1913   Thomas MacDonagh. *Thomas Campion and the Art of English Poetry*. Dublin.

1914   A. Blyth Webster. "Translation from Old into Modern English," *Essays and Studies by the English Association*, 5, 153–171.

1915   Thomas Fitzhugh. "The Origin of Verse," *Bulletin of the School of Latin*. University of Virginia.

1915   Helene Louise Cohen. *The Ballade*. New York: Columbia University Press.

1916   Robert Bridges. *Ibant Obscuri*. Oxford: Clarendon Press.

1918   Gerard Manley Hopkins. *Poems*, ed. with notes by Robert Bridges. London: Humphrey Milford.

1919   Matthew Albert Bayfield. *The Measures of the Poets*. London: Cambridge University Press.

1919   John Livingston Lowes. *Convention and Revolt in Poetry*. Boston: Houghton Mifflin Company.

1919   George Saintsbury. *Some Recent Studies in English Prosody*. London: Oxford University Press.

1920   Herbert L. Creek. "Rising and Falling Rhythm in English Verse," *PMLA*, 35, i (New Series, 28, i), 76–90.

1920   Bliss Perry. *A Study of Poetry*. Boston: Houghton Mifflin Company.

1921   Robert Bridges. *Milton's Prosody*. Final rev.; London: Oxford University Press.

1921   T. S. Omond. *English Metrists*. Oxford: Clarendon Press.

1921   B. de Selincourt. "Rhyme in English Poetry," *Essays and Studies by the English Association*, 7, 7–29.

1922   P. F. Baum. *The Principles of English Versification*. Cambridge, Mass.: Harvard University Press.

1922   George R. Stewart, Jr. *Modern Metrical Technique as Illustrated by Ballad Meter (1700–1920)*. New York: Columbia University Press.

1923   Lascelles Abercrombie. *Principles of English Prosody*. London: Martin Secker.

1923   P. F. Baum. *The Principles of English Versification*. Cambridge: Harvard University Press.

1923   M. W. Croll. "Music and Metrics," *Studies in Philology*, 20, 388–394.

1923   Godfrey Dewey. *Relative Frequency of English Speech Sounds*. Cambridge: Harvard University Press.

1923   T. S. Omond. *Some Thoughts About Verse*. London: Oxford University Press.

1923   Egerton Smith. *The Principles of English Metre*. London: Oxford University Press.

1923 William Thomson. *The Rhythm of Speech*. Glasgow: Maclehose, Jackson.

1923 H. C. K. Wyld. *Studies in English Rhymes from Surrey to Pope*. London: John Murray.

1923 V. Zhirmunsky. *Rifma, ee istoria i teoriya*. Petrograd.

1924 M. W. Croll. *The Rhythm of English Verse*. Ann Arbor: Edwards Brothers

1924 Sydney Grew. *A Book of English Prosody*. London: Grant Richards.

1924 Margery Swett. "Free Verse Again," *Poetry: A Magazine of Verse*, *25* (December), 153–159.

1925 E. A. Sonnenschein. *What Is Rhythm?* Oxford: Basil Blackwell & Mott.

1925 George R. Stewart, Jr. "The Meter of the Popular Ballad," *PMLA*, *40*, 933–962.

1926 Harriet Monroe. *Poets and Their Art*. New York: Macmillan Company.

1926 Louis Untermeyer. *The Forms of Poetry*. New York: Harcourt, Brace, & World.

1927–1936 Robert Bridges. *Collected Essays and Papers*. London: Oxford University Press.

1927 John Livingston Lowes. *The Road to Xanadu*. Boston: Houghton Mifflin Company.

1927 Gilbert Murray. *The Classical Tradition in Poetry*. Cambridge: Harvard University Press. Reprinted by Vintage Books, New York, 1957.

1928 J. C. Andersen. *The Laws of Verse*. London: Cambridge University Press.

1928 Eric Blom. *The Limitations of Music*. London: Macmillan & Co.

1928 Stanley Burnshaw. "Vers-libre in Full Bloom," *Poetry: A Magazine of Verse*, *32* (August), 31–40.

1928 Philip Conrad. "Visual Poetry," *Poetry: A Magazine of Verse*, *32* (May), 112–114.

1928 W. P. Ker. *Form and Style in Poetry*, ed. R. W. Chambers. London: Macmillan & Co.

1928 Sir George Young. *An English Prosody on Inductive Lines*. London: Cambridge University Press.

1929 R. M. Alden. *English Verse: Specimens Illustrating Its Principles and History*. New York: Holt, Rinehart and Winston.

1930 Enid Hamer. *The Metres of English Poetry*. London: Methuen & Co.

1930 Andrew Smithberger and Camille McCole. *On Poetry*. New York: Doubleday.

1930 R. C. Trevelyan. "Classical and English Verse-Structure," *Essays and Studies by the English Association*, 16, 7–25.

1930 Katherine M. Wilson. *Sound and Meaning in English Poetry*. London: Jonathan Cape.

1931 Henry Lanz. *The Physical Basis of Rime*. Stanford.

1932 Lascelles Abercrombie. *Poetry: Its Music and Meaning*. London: Humphrey Milford.

1932 C. E. Andrews. *The Writing and Reading of Verse*. New York: Appleton-Century-Crofts.

1932 William Temple, Archbishop of York. "Poetry and Science," *Essays and Studies by the English Association*, 17, 7–24.

1933 Lascelles Abercrombie. "The Function of Poetry in the Drama," in *English Critical Essays*, ed. Phyllis M. Jones. London: Oxford University Press.

1933 Theodore Maynard. *Preface to Poetry*. New York: Appleton-Century-Crofts.

1933 R. L. Megroz. *Modern English Poetry, 1882–1932: Technical Developments*. London: Ivor Nicholson & Watson.

1934 Gay Wilson Allen. *American Prosody*. New York: American Book Company.

1934 Pallister Barkas. *A Critique of Modern English Prosody (1880–1930)*. Halle, Germany: M. Niemeyer.

1934 Gordon Bottomley. "Poetry and the Contemporary Theatre," *Essays and Studies by the English Association*, 19.

1934 Robert Swann and Frank Sidgwick. *The Making of Verse*. London: Sidgwick & Jackson.

1935 Sir Stanley Leathes. *Rhythm in English Poetry*. London: William Heinemann.

1935 Wilbur L. Schramm. *Approaches to a Science of English Verse*. University of Iowa Studies, Series on Aims and Progress of Research, No. 46.

1935 Allen Tate. "Narcissus as Narcissus," in *Reason in Madness*. New York: G. P. Putnam's Sons.

1935 Ruth Wallerstein. "The Development of the Rhetoric and Metre of the Heroic Couplet, Especially in 1625–1645," *PMLA*, 50, 166–209.

1935 Lawrence John Zillman. *The Elements of English Verse*. New York: Macmillan Company.

1937 Yvor Winters. *Primitivism and Decadence*. New York: Arrow Editions.

1938 Cleanth Brooks, Jr., and Robert Penn Warren. *Understanding Poetry*. New York: Holt, Rinehart and Winston.

1938 Robert Hillyer. *First Principles of Verse*. Boston: The Writer.

1938 Elder Olson. *General Prosody*. Chicago: University of Chicago Press.

1938 John Crowe Ransom. *The World's Body*. New York: Charles Scribner's Sons.

1939 J. E. Bernard, Jr. *The Prosody of the Tudor Interlude*. New Haven: Yale University Press.

1939 André Classe. *The Rhythm of English Prose*. Oxford: Basil Blackwell & Mott.

1939 Max Eastman. *The Enjoyment of Poetry*. New York: Charles Scribner's Sons.

1940 Charles David Abbott. "Poetry in the Making," *Poetry: A Magazine of Verse*, 55 (February), 258–266.

1940 Kenneth Burke. "On Musicality in Verse," *Poetry: A Magazine of Verse*, 57 (October), 31–40.

1941 John Crowe Ransom. *The New Criticism* (Part IV). Norfolk, Conn.: New Directions.

1941 Rose Elizabeth Wright. *Critique of Teaching Literary Forms*. Philadelphia: Dolphin Press.

1942 John C. Pope. *The Rhythm of Beowulf*. New Haven: Yale University Press.

1942 René Wellek and Austin Warren. "Euphony, Rhythm, and Meter," in *Theory of Literature*. New York: Harcourt, Brace & World.

1943 James Craig La Drière. "Prosody," in *Dictionary of World Literature*, ed. Joseph T. Shipley. New York: Philosophical Library.

1944 Cecil Day-Lewis. *Poetry for You*. Oxford: Basil Blackwell & Mott.

1945 Kenneth L. Pike. *The Intonation of American English*. Ann Arbor: University of Michigan Press.

1946 Stephen Spender. "The Making of a Poem," *Partisan Review* (Summer).

1946 Donald A. Stauffer. *The Nature of Poetry*. New York: W. W. Norton & Company.

1947 Sister Mary Cleophas Costello. *Between Fixity and Flux*. Washington, D.C.: Catholic University of America Press

1947 Helen L. Gardner. *Four Quartets: A Commentary*. London: Dennis Dobson.

1947 Sister Marcella Marie Holloway. *The Prosodic Theory of Gerard Manley Hopkins*. Washington, D.C.; Catholic University of America Press.

1948 Charles David Abbott and S. P. Capen. *Poets at Work*. New York: Harcourt, Brace & World.

1948 Karl Shapiro. *English Prosody and Modern Poetry*. Baltimore: Johns Hopkins Press.

1948 Karl Shapiro. *A Bibliography of Modern Prosody*. Baltimore: Johns Hopkins Press.

1948 Yvor Winters. "Foreword," in *Selected Poems of Elizabeth Daryush*. New York: The Swallow Press and William Morrow and Company.

1949 Leo L. Beranek. *Acoustic Measurements*. New York: John Wiley & Sons.

1950 Raymond D. Havens. "Structure and Prosodic Pattern in Shelley's Lyrics," *PMLA*, 65 (December),1076–1087.

1951 Josephine Miles. *The Continuity of Poetric Language*. Berkeley: University of California Press.

1951 Ezra Pound. *A. B. C. of Reading*. Norfolk, Conn.: New Directions.

1951 Edward Sapir. *Selected Writings in Language, Culture, and Personality*, ed. David G. Mandelbaum. Berkeley: University of California Press.

1951 Elizabeth Cox Wright. *Metaphor, Sound, and Meaning in Bridges' 'The Testament of Beauty.'* Philadelphia: University of Pennsylvania Press.

1952 Karl Shapiro. "An A.B.C. of Prosody," in *British Literature from Blake to the Present Day*, ed. Hazelton Spencer, Walter E. Houghton, and Herbert Barrows. Boston: D. C. Heath & Company.

1953 Marjorie Boulton. *The Anatomy of Poetry*. London: Routledge and Kegan Paul.

1953 Melville Cane. *Making a Poem*. New York: Harcourt, Brace & World.

1953 Ants Oras. *Milton's Blank Verse and the Chronology of His Major Poems*. Gainesville: University of Florida Press.

1953 Curt Sachs. *Rhythm and Tempo*. New York: W. W. Norton & Company.

1953 S. E. Sprott. *Milton's Art of Prosody*. Oxford: Blackwell.

1954 Victor Hamm. "Meter and Meaning," *PMLA*, *69* (September–December), 695–710.

1954 Paul M. Roberts. "Intonation," in *Understanding Grammar*. New York: Harper & Row.

1954 Edith Sitwell. "Poetry," in *Cassell's Encyclopoedia of World Literature*, ed. S. H. Steinberg. Vol. I. New York: Funk & Wagnalls.

1955 Eliseo Vivas. *Creation and Discovery*. New York: Noonday Press.

1956 Frederick Eckman. "Karl Shapiro's 'Adam and Eve,'" *Texas Studies in English*, *35*, 1–10.

1956 John Hollander. "The Music of Poetry," *Journal of Aesthetics and Art Criticism*, *15* (December), 232–244.

1956 Arthur Miller. "The Family in Modern Drama," *The Atlantic Monthly* (April), *197*, 35–41.

1956 George L. Trager and Henry Lee Smith, Jr. *An Outline of English Structure*. Washington, D.C.: American Council of Learned Societies.

1956 Joshua Whatmough. *Poetic, Scientific, and Other Forms of Discourse*. Berkeley: University of California Press.

1957 William Beare. *Latin Verse and European Song*. London: Methuen & Co.

1957 Robert Beum. "Syllabic Verse in English," *Prairie Schooner*, *31*, 259–275.

1957 Seymour Chatman. "Linguistics, Poetics, and Interpretation: The Phonemic Dimension," *Quarterly Journal of Speech*, *43* (October).

1957 Northrop Frye, ed. *Sound and Poetry*. English Institute Essays. [Introduction by Frye. Essays by Edward T. Cone, Frederick W. Sternfield, John Hollander, Craig La Drière, Ants Oras, Harold Whitehall.] New York: Columbia University Press.

1958 Frederick Eckman. *Cobras and Cockle Shells: Modes in Recent Poetry*. Flushing, N.Y.: Sparrow Press.

1959 W. K. Wimsatt, Jr., and Monroe C. Beardsley. "The Concept of Meter: An Exercise in Abstraction," *PMLA*, *74* (December), 585–593.

1960 Carol Maddison. *Apollo and the Nine: A History of the Ode*. London: Routledge and Kegan Paul.

1961 Robert Beum. "Yeats's Octaves," *Texas Studies in Literature and Language*, *3*, 89–96.

1961   George Hemphill, ed. *Discussions of Poetry: Rhythm and Sound.* Boston: D. C. Heath & Company.

1961   Jiří Levý. "On the Relations of Language and Stanza Pattern in the English Sonnet," *Worte und Werte, 33,* 214–231.

1961   Sister Mary Augustine Roth. *Coventry Patmore's 'Essay on English Metrical Law': A Critical Edition with a Commentary.* Washington, D.C.: Catholic University of America Press.

1962   Martin Halpern. "On the Two Chief Metrical Modes in English," *PMLA,* 77 (March), 177–186.

1963   Robert Beum. "Some Observations on Spenser's Verse Forms," *Neuphilologische Mitteilungen, 64,* 180–196.

Index